UK SERIAL KILLERS 1930-2021
Their lives, crimes and punishments.

This novel is entirely a work of information searched for, extracted from, researched and collated by the author from information in the public domain.

AUTHOR'S NOTE

Whilst researching this book a few things were found to be very similar in many of the killer's lives. Most of them come from broken families or lower income families and areas of poor housing. Many of the killings involve a sexual element with the killer's need for power over the victim very apparent, which I suppose is why so many victims are female and young, or elderly. Serial killers don't take on grown men. Psychiatrists would no doubt analyse all that and come up with a detailed answer. I can only come up with one, serial killers are a bunch of cowards.

A sobering figure is that the latest official reported figure for missing persons each year is 176,000 of which 76,000 are children and 1 in 10 of those children are from foster homes and care homes. That figure is only of those actually reported to the authorities as missing, the real figure is thought to be much higher.

Are there serial killers out there in the UK now? Of course there are, there's never been a time when one or more weren't operating and I think the chances of that diminishing is a non starter these days with the explosion in social media giving more opportunities for them to groom and meet potential victims.

Be warned, some of the descriptions in this book, although true, are quite upsetting. I have kept away from sensationalism and stuck to the facts. I also left out the 'accidental' serial killers. The ones who didn't actually plan their killings but got caught up in a moment of madness.

Contents in chronological order;

1943 JOHN CHRISTIE

Born to carpet designer Ernest Christie and his wife in Northowram, Halifax on April 8th 1899, John Reginald Halliday Christie was the sixth of seven children. He did very well at school winning a scholarship to Halifax secondary School, was in the Church Choir and the Scouts although he was not a very friendly boy and didn't socialise outside those disciplines. He left school on 22nd April 1913 and took a job as assistant projectionist at a local cinema. He had erectile dysfunction that gained him the nickname 'can't-do-it-Christie' amongst his peers. This affected his later married life although he was able to perform with prostitutes. He served in WW1 as an infantryman and after a mustard gas attack was unable to talk any louder than a whisper.

He married Ethel Simpson from Halifax on May 10th 1920, his impotence not helping their relationship and he continued visiting prostitutes. At this time Christie took to petty crime and spent much of their married life in prison serving sentences for theft, larceny and assault. They separated for four years with Ethel joining her parents in Bradford and Christie moving to London. By 1934 he appeared to have got his life in order and the re-united couple moved into a ground floor flat at 10 Rillington Place in Notting Hill, London, a run-down three story terrace in a working class area where the tenants had no bathrooms and all shared one outside toilet. It was built beside the above-ground section of the Metropolitan Line which would have been deafening every time a train went past. Christie took a job at the Commodore Cinema in Hammersmith and at the start of WW2 he joined the War Reserve Police Force. How he got in with a prison record is not known. He worked out of Harrow Road police station where he met Gladys Jones with whom he had an affair as her husband was away in the army. On his return the husband sort out Christie and assaulted him.

Christie's murders were committed over a 10 year period between 1943 and 1953. His MO was to somehow make his chosen victims unconscious with domestic gas, rape them and then strangle them.

His first murder was committed when he was 44, she was a prostitute called Ruth Fuerst age 21 who Christie took back to his home on August 24th 1943 when his wife was away visiting her relatives. Christie strangled Fuerst with a rope and kept her body under the floorboards of the living room for a day before burying it in the small unkempt tenement back garden.

Moving onto a new job as a clerk at a radio factory in Acton Christie selected his second victim from the staff who worked there. She was Muriel Eady and suffered from bronchitis. On 7th October 1944 Christie persuaded her he had a new cure for the ailment at his home and when she went there he persuaded her to inhale from a jar of Friar's Balsam into which he had inserted a pipe from the domestic gas supply in the flat. In those days the domestic gas supply was coal gas with 15% carbon monoxide content. He turned on the gas and Eady passed out. He then raped her and strangled her burying the body in the back yard next to Ruth Fuerst.

New tenants, the Evans, moved into the upper flat at number 10 Rillington Place, Timothy and his wife Beryl, who soon produced a baby daughter Geraldine. By December 1949 both Beryl and Geraldine were missing. The police search found both bodies wrapped in a blanket together with a 16 week old male foetus in an outdoor washhouse with Beryl's body showing signs of having been assaulted prior to her murder. Christie was interviewed and pointed the finger at Timothy Evans recounting how he had often heard violent arguments between the couple and seen bruises on Beryl's face during the time they had been lodging at 10 Rillington Place. Evans denied the murders and said that he thought his wife had become pregnant and not told him but she may have asked Christie to perform an illegal abortion which had gone wrong and that accounted for the foetus with the bodies. Christie had made it known to local women that he was an abortionist, a total lie, but he may have thought it might gain their confidence for getting them to his flat in the future. The police believed Christie, probably because as an ex war reserve policeman they looked on him as one of their own, and they arrested Timothy Evans on charges of murdering his wife and child. He was found guilty and hung in March 1950.

Three years passed and Christie had a job with British Road Services at their Shepherd's Bush depot as a clerk. The vacant two floors at 10 Rillington Place were filled by black immigrants of the Windrush generation that Christie and his wife disliked. He showed racist overtones and managed to get sole access and exclusive use of the small back garden from the council housing department after Ethel prosecuted one of the neighbours for assault arguing that it gave him space between them and their neighbours. More than likely he was afraid of the burials coming to light as they were shallow and already his dog had unearthed Eady's skull which Christie had taken and left inside a bombed out house in St Mark's Road a few streets away.

On December 14th 1952 Christie strangled his wife in their bed and sold her belongings. He was by now unemployed again and living on unemployment benefit of £3.12s a week. On 26th January he forged his wife's signature and took out all the money in her bank account. He told various stories about her absence saying she had moved out and gone to Birmingham, or Sheffield or taken up with another man.

Between January and March 1953 Christie invited at least 3 more prostitutes to his flat at Rillington Place where he gassed them, raped them and strangled them. They were Kathleen Maloney, Rita Nelson and Hectorina McLennan.

On 20th March 1953 Christie moved out of 10 Rillington Place after fraudulently sub-letting it to a young couple. On the same evening that he left the landlord visited for Christies unpaid rent and found the new 'tenants' and demanded they leave the following day. He then allowed the top floor tenant, Beresford Brown, to move down into the flat. Christies last three victims were discovered when the new tenant tried to put a shelf up in the kitchen. As he screwed into the wall it revealed it was not a real wall but layers of thick wallpaper stuck onto each other and it gave way and revealed the three bodies of Maloney, Nelson and McLennan. A police search found the two bodies he had buried in the garden and his wife's body under the floorboards in the front room.

After leaving Rillington Place Christie went to Rowton House, a Hostel for unemployed men in Kings Cross where he booked in for a week but left after 4 nights when the news of the gruesome discovery at 10 Rillington Place made the papers. He wandered around London sleeping rough and spending most days in cafes or cinemas. He pawned his watch for 10s and was arrested by a policeman moving on vagrants near Putney Bridge who asked him for some identity. In his pockets were a few coins, a wallet, his marriage certificate, ration book, union card and a newspaper clipping about Timothy Evans.

Christie was arrested and tried for murder for which he was given the death sentence. His trial began on 22nd June 1953 in the same courtroom that had tried Timothy Evans three years earlier. Christie pleaded insanity and claimed not to remember the events or of killing anybody. The jury rejected that plea and took just 85 minutes to find him guilty. He was hung at 9am on July 15th 1953 in Pentonville Prison and buried within its precincts. His executioner was Albert Pierrepoint, Englands last executioner who had executed up to 600 people. His father and grandfather had the job before him.

It is now accepted that Timothy Evans was hung in error and his conviction was quashed in 2004. Not much good to him.

Christie may well have murdered more women as he had a fetish for collecting clumps of his victim's pubic hair. Only one of the four clumps in his possession that were found at 10 Rillington Place matched any of his victims although Fuerst and Eady's bodies had decomposed too far to be checked when found in the back garden. One clump matched his wife's hair type but that leaves one unaccounted for if two were in fact Fuerst and Eady's.

****

1946 JOHN BODKIN ADAMS

The Scotland Yard files on this case were closed to the public after Adams's trial in 1957 and would remain so until 2033 when a request to re-open them by Historian Pamela Cullen in 2003 was given permission for them to be released into the public domain.

Adams was born 21st January 1899 in Randalstown, Ulster, Ireland. His father Samuel was a preacher and skilled watchmaker. The family were very religious and members of the Plymouth Brethren. Samuel married Ellen Bodkin in 1896 when he was thirty-nine and she was thirty. John was the eldest of their two sons. Adam's father died in 1914 of a stroke and his brother in 1918 of influenza. Adams education was normal he didn't excel at anything and was considered pretty 'run-of-the-mill' by his teachers at school and at university. In 1921 he gained a position as 'assistant houseman' at the Bristol Royal Infirmary. He was there a year and moved onto be a general practitioner in a Christian Practice in Eastbourne, Sussex in 1922 living with his mother and his cousin, Sarah Florence Henry. In 1929 he borrowed £2000 (£200,000 at today's equivalent) from William Mawhood, a patient of his and bought an eighteen room mansion called Kent Lodge in Seaside Road (now re-named Trinity Trees) Eastbourne. He began expanding his involvement with the Mawhoods by turning up at mealtimes with his mother and cousin expecting to be invited to join the table. He even charged items to the Mawhood's accounts at local shops without their permission. William Mawhood died in 1949 and although not attending the funeral Adams visited the widow to pay his respects and, without asking, took a 22 carat gold pen as a 'memoir' of her husband. That was the last time he visited Mrs Mawhood and the £2,000 loan remained unpaid. By now the local grape-vine had started buzzing with unsubstantiated accusations about Adam's patient relationships back in the 1930s. In 1935 he inherited £7,385 (£430,000 today) from former patient Matilda Whitton who's total estate only amounted to £11,465. The will was contested by the relatives but upheld in court. In 1941 Adams put patient Agnes Pike on a selection of drugs which he injected including morphine. Pike's health deteriorated and the owner of the hotel she lived in full time alerted her relatives who called in another doctor who found no reason for Mrs Pike to be on any course of drugs, especially not morphine. The morphine had reduced Mrs Pike's mental capacity to such an extent she could not recall her own name or age. The relatives took her off Adams list and she made a full recovery after 2 months. In 1941 Adams gained a diploma in anaesthetics and worked one day a week at the local hospital where his 'skills' were avoided as much as possible by the staff as he managed too often to mix up the gases and even fall asleep during operations. In 1943 his mother passed away and in 1952 his cousin had developed cancer and died just thirty minutes after Adams had given her a pain relief injection.

Adam's career was a very successful one with his reputation as 'the wealthiest doctor in England' opening many doors for him. He was personal physician to a host of elite and wealthy people including lower Royals and top businessmen in his Eastbourne area. After years of the local 'grape-vine' accusations and being the financial recipient in 132 of his patients' wills the local police acted in 1956 after a call from Leslie Henson a celebrated music hall performer about the unexpected death of his friend Gertrude Hullett who died unexpectedly whilst in Adam's care. The first local post mortem stated that her death did not appear to be natural. A second post mortem by a Home Office Pathologist gave the cause of death as barbiturate poisoning. Officers from Scotland Yard were called in to take over the investigation from the Eastbourne Police. They had a clear suspect in Adams but needed to link him with hard evidence to the charge that he had murdered patients for their money after persuading them to put him in their wills. They concentrated on the deaths of Adam's patients in the decade 1946 to 1956 with 310 Death Certificates and patient records taken away for close examination by the Home Office Pathologists who considered 163 needed further examination. These 163 were all elderly patients of Adams and all had passed away whilst in a coma which pointed to them having been subjected to a narcotic or barbiturate injection to bring that on. Statements were taken from the nursing staff who worked with Adams and from the deceased patients' relatives. Not many had any good words for his demeanour and nurses told of being asked to leave the room prior to him injecting patients whilst relatives were prevented from contacting them.

The BMA (British Medical Association) sent a letter to all the doctors practising in Eastbourne at the time reminding them of their patient confidentiality if interviewed by the police. The BMA was obviously worried that one of their members could be a mass murderer. Most of the doctors in the area who had had dealings with patients that Adams took over that had then died took little notice of the letter, ignored it and gave statements to the police about those deceased patients. The Attorney General of the day Sir Reginald Manningham-Butler was incensed by the BMA action and took a copy of the Yard's report about Adams to the BMA President who dropped their advice the next day after reading it.

DS Herbert Hannam of the Yard was leading the enquiry and interviewed Adams asking why so many dead patients left him money? Adams answered that it was because he never charged them any fees and they felt guilty. When asked why Adams had lied on the cremation forms, where a doctor signing the death certificate must state if he was to inherit from the deceased, Adams said he just wanted the cremations to go along smoothly for the relatives and the amounts were very small.

A search of Adams house was made by Hannam and DI Pugh of Eastbourne CID on 24th November 1956 using a warrant issued under the Dangerous Drugs Act of 1951. When asked for his drugs register Adams revealed that he had not kept one since 1949. During the search he was seen to slip two small medicine bottles into his pocket which turned out to be morphine. Later that year the police were made aware or rumours of a homosexual liaison between 'a police officer, a magistrate and a doctor' in Eastbourne. The magistrate was Sir Roland Gwynne, the Mayor of Eastbourne 1929-31, brother of the MP Rupert Gwynne. Roland Gwynne was a regular visitor to Adams's home every morning at 9am and they frequently went on holiday together. The police officer allegedly involved was Richard Walker the Chief Constable of Eastbourne. Hannam chose not to pursue this line of enquiry despite homosexuality being an offence in 1956.

Adams was arrested on December 19th 1956. Hannam had sufficient hard evidence in four cases to proceed and chose to bring murder charges on two, the murders of Edith Alice Morrell and Gertrude Hullett.

Morrell was a wealthy widow and was partially paralyzed by a stroke. She also suffered severe arthritis. Adams had given her doses of heroin and morphine 'to help her sleep' during the ten months prior to her death with medical evidence stating that the amounts listed on Adam's prescriptions for Morrell in the five days between 7th and 12th of November would have been enough to kill her let alone tenth months worth. Morrell made several wills with Adams receiving large amounts of money in some and very little in others. She died on 13th November 1950 leaving Adams a small amount of money, a Rolls Royce car and a chest of silver ware. He also helped himself to an infra red lamp Morrell had bought for herself. On the day of her death Adams arranged for a cremation stating on the form that he had 'no pecuniary interest in the death of the deceased'. This meant no post-mortem would happen and the cremation could go ahead immediately. Morrell's ashes were scattered at sea the same evening.

Gertrude Hullet died aged 50 on 23rd July 1956 having been prescribed large amounts of sodium barbitone and sodium phenobarbitone by Adams to ease her depression which she suffered with since her husband's death four months earlier. She had relapsed into a coma on the 19th and was attended by a Doctor Harris as Adams was unavailable until later that day. On attending Adams didn't mention the medication he had put Hullet on and after her death Dr Harris called in a pathologist who took an example of her spinal fluid. He suspected narcotic poisoning and asked for a stomach sample which Adams refused. However a urine sample showed Hullet had 115 grains of sodium barbitone in her body, twice that of a fatal dose. Adams was a beneficiary in Hullet's will being left another Rolls Royce, which he immediately sold for around £3000 and a cheque for £1000 which he had 'specially cleared' into his account in one day.

The trial of the Morrell case was a very involved affair with the defence managing to convince the jury that no evidence showed a murder had been committed let alone a murder by Adams. This was supported by the expert witnesses for the prosecution who stated when questioned under oath that they couldn't be one percent sure Adam's actions had caused her death. He was found not guilty and acquitted on 15th April 1957 and the judge threw out the Hullett case at the same time.

It is worth looking at some of the testimonial evidence that Hannam gathered about other Adam patients which never got to court and has been locked away until 2003. It does throw suspicion on Adams.

August 1939, Adam's patient Agnes Pike's worsening condition raised worries with her solicitors who called in another Doctor, Dr Matthew to take over the treatment. Matthew examined Pike with Adams present and could find no illness or disease in the patient other than she seemed 'under the influence of prescribed drugs' causing her to be incoherent and unaware of her surroundings. Dr Matthew took over the patient and found that Adams had also banned all Pike's relatives from seeing her which he found unusual. He withdrew all Adams medications and Pike regained her full facilities in a few weeks.

February 1950, Adam's patient Amy Ware died aged 76. Adams had banned her from seeing her relatives. She left him £1000 from her £9000 estate. Adams stated on the cremation certificate that he had no 'pecuniary interest in the deceased'. He was charged and convicted for this falsehood in 1957.

December 1950, Adam's patient Annabelle Kilgour died aged 89. She had been with Adams since suffering a stroke in that June. The nurse involved in her care told police that she was 'certain Adams gave her the wrong injections and a far too concentrated type of barbiturate.' She left Adams £200 and a clock.

May 1952 Adam's patient Julia Bradnum died aged 85. The year before Adams had persuaded her that to leave her house to her relatives would create 'sharing' problems and he had accompanied her to her solicitors where she changed her will so the house would be sold and the money split. She also made him her executor. He received £661. The day before she died she had been doing her housework and going out for a walk seemingly as right as rain. The next morning she felt unwell and Adams was called. He gave her an injection telling a nurse 'it will be over in three minutes.' It was. Adams confirmed her to be dead and left the house. The body was exhumed in 1956 and the pathologist could find no evidence of the 'cerebal haemorrage' that Adams had put on the death certificate as the cause of death.

November 1952, Adam's patient Julia Thomas aged 72 was being treated for depression after her cat died. On the 19th Adams gave her sedatives so she would feel 'better in the morning'. The next day the 20th he gave her more tablets and she went into a coma. On the 21st he gave more tablets and told the cook that 'Mrs Thomas has promised me the typewriter, I'll take it now.' Which he did. She died early the next morning.

January 1953, Adam's patient Hilda Neil Miller 86, died in a hotel where she permanently lived with her sister Clara. Adams had refused to allow their relatives to visit for many months and it seemed they did not receive their post either. A close friend Dolly Wallis did visit and couldn't see what was wrong with Hilda. She noticed that when Adams was there he took small articles from the rooms and pocketed them. Adams arranged the funeral and burial himself.

February 1954 Clara Neil Miller sister of the deceased Hilda Neil Miller died aged 87 in the same hotel. Dolly Wallis asked why Adams locked the bedroom door when he attended to Clara and he said he was assisting her in 'personal matters'. Clara also appeared to be under the influence of drugs. A nurse attending Clara stated to Hannam when he was investigating Adams that she once entered Clara's room unnoticed to close the windows on a particularly cold winter day and found her near naked on the bed with the windows wide open and Adams reading to her loudly from the Bible. Clara left Adams £1,275 and he charged her estate a further £700 after her death. He was her sole executor and arranged the funeral where only he and the hotel owner Annie Sharpe, who received £200 in the will, were present.

May 1955 James Downs the brother-in-law of Amy Ware died aged 88. Adams was treating him for a broken ankle at a nursing home and prescribing a sedative containing morphia. On 7th April Adams told the nurse to give Downs a tablet to make him more alert and two hours later arrived with a solicitor to amend Down's will into Adam's favour to the tune of £1000. Downs died in a coma 36 hours after Adams visit. Adams charged Down's estate £216 for his 'services' and signed the cremation form as 'no pecuniary interest in the death of the deceased.'

March 1956 Adam's patient Alfred John Hullett aged 71died. He was the husband of Gertrude Hullett. After his death Adams visited a chemist and bought a 10cc hypodermic solution of morphine in Hullett's name which contained 5 grains of morphine and asked for the prescription to be back dated to the previous day. Hannam presumed this was to cover the morphine Adams had already injected Hullet with, which was from his own stock. Hullett left Adams £500 in his will.

November 1956 Adam's patient Annie Sharpe, the owner of the hotel where the Neil Millers died, and a major witness in any prosecution of Adams, died of 'carcinomatosis of the peritoneal cavity' during the police investigations into Adams. Adams had diagnosed that she had cancer just five days before and prescribed hyperduric morphine and 36 pethidine tablets. Hannam had interviewed Sharpe and thought she would be a key witness for the prosecution of murder charges against Adams. It was not to be and she was cremated.

After his acquittal Adams resigned from the NHS and later that year was convicted of 8 counts of forging prescriptions, 4 counts of making false statements on cremation forms and 3 offences under the Dangerous Drugs Act. He was also fined £2,400 plus costs and struck of the medical register by the BMA. He sold his story to the Daily Express for £10,000 and sued other newspapers for libel based on the 'not guilty' verdict. He stayed in Eastbourne but was shunned by the residents who had a common belief that he had indeed murdered 21 people.

Adams was unbelievably re-instated as a GP in 1961 and resumed his career although patients were hard to come by. He applied for a visa to America in 1962 to seek pastures new but it was refused. He died aged 84 in 1983 after slipping over and fracturing his hip. Taken to Eastbourne hospital he developed a chest infection and died on 4th July of left ventricular failure. He left an estate of £402,970. He had been receiving legacies right up to his death.

The number of people he killed is anything between 0 and 163 plus

****

1951 JOHN STRAFFEN

John Thomas Straffen 1930-2007 was born in Borden Military camp in Hampshire where his father was serving in the Army. The family then spent six years in India and returned in 1938 whereupon his father took a discharge and the family settled in Bath, Somerset. John was referred to social services in October of that year for truancy and stealing and in June 1939 given two years probation for purse theft. He was taken to a psychiatrist and certified as mental defective and in 1940 given an IQ of 58 and a mental age of six, he was 10 at the time. He was sent to a residential school for mentally defective children in Sambourne, Warkwickshire and then on to a senior school at Besford Court. His records show he was violent and abusive. At 14 he was suspected of strangling two geese. At 16 his review put his IQ at 64 and his mental age at 9 and somehow he was recommended for discharge? He returned home to Bath, to an overcrowded tenement and took a job as a machinist in a clothing factory. He started stealing from houses and hiding whatever he took. In July

1947 he was reported to the police by a 13 year old girl for assaulting her and threatening to kill her. Six weeks later he strangled a flock of five chickens belonging to the girl's father and was arrested. During his interviews he confessed to burglaries about which the police knew nothing, he was remanded in custody and Medically examined at HM Prison Horfield where he was pronounced as mentally retarded and admitted to Hortham open prison in Bristol where he was well behaved and a model prisoner. He was then transferred to a low security agricultural hostel in Winchester. He soon fell back into his old theft ways and was returned to Hortham in 1950 and made things worse by absconding and resisting the police when they came to take him back. He was assessed again in 1951 and the Medical Officer for Bath found an improvement to a mental age of ten and recommended he be assessed every 6 months. On the very morning of that assessment Straffen murdered a young girl named Christine Butcher. It has been suggested that the press coverage of that police hunt for the killer reacted well with Straffen who wanted to cause the police as much trouble as he could. On July 15th 1951 he went to the cinema in Bath on his own passing 1 Camden Crescent and saw 5 year old Brenda Goddard who lived there with her foster parents. He lifted her over a fence on the pretext of picking flowers and strangled her before continuing to the cinema to watch the film Shockproof and returning home afterwards.

The police interviewed him although at that time they didn't have him down as violent. His employer who was not aware of his mental record was visited by the police as a matter of course to confirm his employment and then sacked Straffen as a result of that information. On 8th August he met 9 year old Cicely Batstone at the cinema and went on the bus with her to a meadow known locally as the Tumps and strangled her. There were many witnesses who had seen the pair together including the bus conductor who was an old work mate of Straffen and a courting couple who had watched them for a time and realised who they had seen when the alarm was raised by the police the next day when they began looking for Cicely. They took the police to the place and her body was found.

The police arrested Straffen that day and he confessed to both killing Cicely and Brenda. On medical evidence from the medical officer at Horfield Prison the jury returned a verdict that Straffen was insane and unfit to plead. He was sent to Broadmoor Hospital in Berkshire, then officially called a 'Lunatic Asylum' and renamed as a Hospital by the Ministry of Health when they took it over in 1948 and prisoners were then re-labelled as 'patients'

On 29th April 1952 Straffen scaled the ten foot high perimeter wall during a work detail whilst concealing civilian clothes beneath his prison suit. Five hours later he strangled 5 year old Linda Bowyer who was riding her bicycle in nearby Farley Hill and he was caught soon after but before the police were aware of the killing. He told them 'I did not kill the little girl on the bicycle' and the next morning the police found her body. He was charged with the murder and remanded to Brixton Prison. Broadmoor installed a system of high pitch wailing sirens to alert the local population of any future escapes as a result of Straffen's escape and murder of Linda. The trial was on 21st July 1952 and the jury returned a verdict of guilty and the death sentence was passed. The execution was set for September 4th but he was reprieved.

He was moved to HM Prison Wandsworth in1952 and then to Horfield in1956 after an escape attempt was discovered at Wandsworth. In 1958 due to the continual petitioning of the residents of Bristol and Bath against having him near them he was sent to HM Prison Cardiff. Then in 1966 he was transferred again to a high security wing at HM Prison Parkhurst and then in May 1968 onto top security wing E at HM Prison Durham with fellow child killer Ian Brady. 1994 Home Secretary Michael Howard put Straffen on the whole life tariff. He died in Durham in November 2007 age 77 having set the British record for being in prison of 55 years.

****

1956 PETER MANUEL

An American by birth Peter Manuel was born in New York on 26th March 1926 and at aged just 5 his Scottish parents decided to move back to Scotland and settled in Motherwell. The young Manuel was a persistent problem to the local police and went to prison at age 15 for a string of sexual assaults. At 20 he attacked and raped a female and received a 9 year sentence at Peterhead Prison being released early in 1953 aged 27. He started a relationship in Glasgow with Ann O'Hara and they were going to marry in July 1955 but at the last moment O'Hara found out about his criminal past and the sex assaults and broke off the engagement. So angry was Manuel at this that he seized 29 year old Mary McLaughlin and threatened her with decapitation. She luckily escaped and later would be able to provide evidence of his violent behaviour at his murder trial.

Manuel started killing on 26th January 1956 which would end 2 years later with 9 people slain. His first victim was Anne Kneilands who he followed onto the East Kilbride Golf Club in Calderwood, raped her, battered her to death with a iron club and dumped her body in the rough next to the 5th tee where it lay for 2 days before being discovered. Manuel was arrested and questioned but his father gave him an alibi.

In September 1956, whilst out on bail for housebreaking, Manuel broke into the Burnside house of Marion Watt, her sister and teenage daughter Vivienne and shot all 3 dead as they lay in their beds. He sexually assaulted Vivienne before killing her. They were discovered the next morning by their domestic cleaner. The police were sure Marion's husband was the killer and although he was away on a fishing trip at the time and would have had to drive 90 miles to the house, fake a break-in, commit three murders and drive 90 miles back by dawn he was charged on the slim evidence that he was seen on the ferry that evening and also seen driving close to his home. He was held on remand at HMP Barlinnie where Manuel was being held at the same time on house breaking charges. Both were being represented by the defence lawyer Laurence Dowdall who had a reputation for finding the smallest flaw in the prosecution evidence and taking full advantage of it. The police soon realised that Watt was totally innocent and released him. Manuel would confess to the killings at a later interview. Manual served 18 months for housebreaking at that time and was released in November 1957 and continued killing. His next victim, although there has always been a question mark as to whether Manuel was the actual killer, was taxi driver Sydney Dunn 36, murdered in December in Newcastle where Manuel had travelled to look for work. Dunn was shot in the head and had his throat cut with his body being found on moorland in Northumberland. Ballistic forensics were not yet at the stage where they could match the gun that killed Dunn to that used in the Watts murders and the MO didn't match Manuel's of housebreaking followed by sexual assault and murder. Plus Dunn was male and the murder occurred outside Scotland. A month later, on 28th December 1957, 17 year old Isabelle Cooke was abducted as she travelled from her Mount Vernon home to a disco at Uddingston Grammar

School. Her body was found raped and strangled in a field. Just 4 days later on New Years Day 1958 Manuel shot the Smart family, Peter, Doris and their 10 year old son Michael at their home in Uddingston. Manuel stayed in the house for a week after killing them, eating their Xmas left-over food and even feeding their cat. This raised Manuel's statistics to 9 murders in just 2 years. Although the police were convinced Manuel was the killer they had no hard evidence until he let his guard down and made a stupid mistake by stealing new banknotes from Peter Smart's wage packet and using them to pay for drinks locally which alerted the police who arrested him and linked the banknotes through the issuing bank to Peter Smart's company. Manuel was arrested and confessed to all 9 murders only to retract the confession once in Court in Glasgow on 12th May 1958 saying that he had been coerced in them by the police. He also dismissed his lawyers on the ninth day of the trial and represented himself. He was found guilty of 8 murders and acquitted of the ninth, the murder of Anne Kneitlands, due to lack of hard evidence. He was hung at 8am on Friday July 11th 1958.

****

1961 GRAHAM YOUNG

Born in Neasden, London on September 7th 1947 to Fred and Bessie Young, Graham was semi-orphaned at 3 months when his mother died of tuberculosis. Fred couldn't cope with Graham and his elder sister Winifred and Graham was put into the care of his aunt Winnie with his sister moving in with the grandparents. His life was upset again when his father remarried in 1950 and took the children back to live in St Albans with him and Molly, his new wife. Graham became a solitary person keeping his own company and not socialising with others of his own age. It was later revealed that he took an interest in real crime murders and read many books on the murderers and their modus operandi. In his teens he embraced Nazi culture and took to wearing swastikas and putting forward his pro Hitler stance claiming the fuehrer was just 'misunderstood'. He also took an interest in the occult and tried to involve local children in ceremonies to call up the Devil and on one occasion sacrificed a cat. At school his only interests were chemistry, forensic science and toxicology. The limited coverage of these subjects available at school was supplemented by him reading books on the subjects and his father encouraging him by buying a chemistry set. By the age of 13 his advanced knowledge of toxicology convinced local chemists he was older and was a capable student which led them to sell him antimony, digitalis and arsenic poison for his 'studying' plus the heavy metal thallium.

Young's first victim was a fellow science pupil, Christopher Williams to whom Young secretly administered a cocktail of poisons that Williams was lucky to survive. Such was the mix that medical experts at William's hospital were unable to name the contents and were quite baffled as to what had happened to Williams. Then Young started using his own family as guinea pigs. When they all started to show signs of poisoning, vomiting, stomach cramps and pain his father suspected that Young might be inadvertently causing it by careless use of his growing chemistry set and number of chemicals he had. The idea that the poisoning was a deliberate act didn't cross his mind at that stage, especially as

Young himself had suffered illness. It is unclear whether this was a false illness to throw people off the scent that he was deliberately poisoning his family or whether he had inadvertently drunk from the wrong tea cup himself.

Young's father's suspicions were again raise when his sister, Winifred, was diagnosed as being poisoned by belladonna in 1961 after collapsing on her way to work. Again the father kept his suspicions to himself and took no action. Young blamed Winifred's illness on the fact that she had mixed shampoo in the teacups and not cleaned them well enough. Young targeted his step-mother in 1962 and she became more and more ill until on April 21st she was rushed to hospital and died that night. The cause of death was wrongly diagnosed as a prolapsed spine and she was cremated at Young's suggestion with no toxicology post mortem. Later it was established that she had developed a tolerance to the antimony Young was putting in her tea and so he had added thallium the night before her death to hasten her end. After his wife's death Fred began to show symptoms of poisoning himself that became so severe that he was hospitalised and diagnosed with antimony poisoning. He refused to believe it was his son but an astute chemistry teacher at Young's school, who had been suspicious for some time, alerted the police on finding poisons and books on poisons in Young's school desk. In police interviews Young's fascination and knowledge of poisons became obvious and he was arrested on May 23rd 1962. He admitted poisoning his father, sister and Christopher William but no murder charge could be levelled at him for the murder of his mother as the evidence was destroyed during her cremation. Young was sent to Broadmoor maximum security hospital for 15 years. He was, at 14, the youngest inmate. Within a short time of his arrival John Berridge, another inmate, dies of cyanide poisoning. Young laid claim to the death saying he had extracted the cyanide from laurel bush leaves in the prison grounds. This was not taken seriously and the cause of Berridge's death was recorded as suicide although where he would have got the cyanide from was never established. Other incidents including sugar soap being put in the warder's tea urn were recorded as happening during Young's time at Broadmoor. He was watched very closely but still managed to increase his knowledge on poisons by reading books on them when left unguarded. Seemingly cured of his obsession Young was released on February 4th 1971 even after telling a nurse that he intended to kill one person a year for every year he had been incarcerated. This comment was recorded in his file but not taken seriously.

On his release he moved into an ex prisoner's hostel and made contact with his sister Winifred who was quite relaxed about meeting him but his father refused. Winifred was worried that Young would visit his old haunts in Neasden and being quite egoistic take delight if recognised by the public. He made several trips to London and bought antimony, thallium and various other poisons. Trevor Sparkes, another hostel resident was soon suffering stomach cramps and sickness whilst another experienced such agony over a period of time that he took his own life. Amazingly no connection to Young was made in either cases. Young took a quartermaster's job at John Holland Laboratories in Bovington, Hertfordshire. His employers were aware of his Broadmoor stay but not of the reasons. Thallium was used in the photographic process at the laboratories. It is not known whether Young stole any but at the time he already had quite a stock in his room bought from London pharmacies. He volunteered as tea boy at John Holland which raised no concerns. His boss Bob Egle 59 began to have stomach cramps and dizziness which was attributed to a local illness known as the Bovington Bug. Other workers experienced cramps but not as severe as Egle who recovered when he stayed at home but became ill again when he returned to work. He died in agony in hospital on July 7th 1971 with his death recorded as pneumonia. Employee Fred Biggs 60, started to show the same symptoms as Egle as did half the workforce in varying degrees. The authorities were called in and attributed the illness to either water contamination, radioactivity or a leakage of chemicals the company used in its production line. Fred Biggs was admitted to the London Hospital for Nervous Diseases and died November 19th 1971. Young made a note in his diary at the time and wrote he was not happy that Biggs had taken so long to die.

The second death at the firm raised questions. About 70 employees had recorded similar symptoms of illness and there were fears for their personal safety at the plant. The company doctor set a reassuring tone at a staff meeting but was surprised when Young challenged him as to why thallium poisoning had not been considered as its use in the photographic process is well known. The doctor was surprised at Young's knowledge and alerted the management who alerted the police. Young's past conviction was brought to light and at his hostel room police found many poisons and his diaries recording the exact doses given to individuals at the factory, their reactions over time and the alterations to the doses.

Young was arrested in Sheerness, Kent on November 21st 1971 where he had been on a visit to his father. A quantity of thallium was found on his person so perhaps his father had been very lucky. When interviewed Young admitted the poisonings but would not sign a written admission of guilt. His trial at St Alban's Crown Court started on June 19th 1972 with him being charged on two counts of murder, two of attempted murder and two of poisoning. He pleaded not guilty to all the charges knowing that his previous convictions could not be entered into evidence and he was not the only person at the John Holland Works that could have poisoned Egle and Biggs. His ego was not admired by the jury or the press. He was arrogant and put on a sinister facade towards the packed public gallery. He was not happy when the press labelled him 'The Teacup Killer.' wishing for a more 'hard' nickname.

The forensic science advances and the cold-bloodied excerpts from his diary had him in a corner and the jury found him guilty of all charges on 29th June 1972 for which he was sentenced to four life sentences. The jury recommended an urgent review of the laws regarding the sale of poisons to the public.

Young was taken to the maximum-security prison at Parkhurst on the Isle of Wight where the UK's most dangerous and serious criminals with mental conditions are housed. Here he built a friendship with Moors Murderer Ian Brady spending time together playing chess and discussing their mutual fascination with Nazi Germany. Young even grew a Hitler moustache. He was very happy when Madame Tussaud's Chamber of Horrors added a waxwork of him alongside his boyhood hero, Dr Crippen.

Young died in his cell on August 1st 1990 aged just 42. The death certificate lists heart failure as the cause but solid rumours remain that fellow inmates, except Brady, were not happy with Young and thought he might poison them so they poisoned him first.

****

1963 IAN BRADY

On the 2nd January 1938 Margaret Stewart, an unmarried waitress in Glasgow had a son, Ian Duncan Stewart, seventeen years he took the surname Brady when his mother married Patrick Brady. His real father's identity has never been positively made although his mother said it was a Glasgow newspaper reporter who died before the birth. The young Stewart had little family support and was taken by into care by the council and put with Mary and John Sloan who had four children of their own. Stewart became known as Ian Sloan. His birth mother made frequent visits and the Sloan family moved to a bigger council house on an estate at Pollock where he was accepted at the highly respected Shawlands Academy which took pupils of above average IQ.

His general behaviour then slipped downwards and twice he was before a juvenile court for burglary. At 15 he left Shawlands and took a menial job at Harland and Wolf shipyard in Govan. He left after a few months and worked as a butcher's messenger. He had a girlfriend called Eve Grant who ended the relationship after Sloan threatened her with a knife after she had gone dancing with another boy. Just before his 17th birthday he was put on probation after being sent to court with 9 charges against him. The condition of having probation and not a prison term was that he live with his real mother who had moved to Manchester and married an Irish fruit importer Patrick Brady who got Ian a job as a market fruit porter and at that point he took the Brady surname.

It didn't take Brady long to break probation and get 3 months in Strangeways for theft of lead from the market. He was sentenced to 2 years in a borstal and 3 months in Latchmere House in London and then at Hatfield Bortsall in Yorkshire. He was found drunk on own brewed alcohol and sent to a tougher unit in Hull. He seems to have altered his ways whilst there and when he was released he completed a course on Book-keeping and in 1959 got a clerical job at Millwards, a wholesale chemical company in Gorton. Whilst there we get an idea of where his mind was going as he read books including

Teach Yourself German, Mein Kampf and others on Nazi propaganda and atrocities.

MYRA HINDLEY

Born in Crumpsall 23rd July 1942 and raised in Gorton. Her father was ex service and an alcoholic who regularly beat her as a child and instilled in her to not let anyone beat her in a fight. She had an awful episode in her early teens when her best friend Michael Higgins drowned in a reservoir. Hindley who was a good swimmer was going to be with him but decided to go elsewhere with another friend that day and blamed herself for Michael's death. Her first job was as an errand clerk at a local engineers'. She was briefly engaged but called it off. She was sacked for absenteeism from the engineering works after six months.

WITH BRADY In January 1961 Hindley joined Millwards as a typist, Brady was already working there and for some reason she became infatuated with him even though his criminal record was well known, perhaps that was the attraction? Their first date was to go to the cinema in December

1961 with Hindley's diary telling of her continuing fascination with him. Their relationship grew and cinema visits were usually to X rated films. They also spent time reading aloud to each other from books detailing Nazi atrocities and Hitler's thoughts and ideas on gaining an Aryan state for German. Hindley seems to have taken to this as she bleached her hair blonde and used a bright crimson lipstick. Brady was taking over her mind and in her parole submission in 1978 she says 'Brady had convinced me there was no God. He could have told me the earth was flat, the moon made of cheese and the sun rose in the west and I would have believed him'

Her personality changed and she began wearing boots and short skirts and leather jackets and together with Brady she ignored their work colleagues and spent every minute they could together. Library records show they borrowed many books on philosophy, crime and torture. She often hired a van in which they planned bank robberies even casing potential banks but nothing ever came of that. She befriended George Clitheroe the President of the Cheadle Rifle Club and visited local ranges. Clitheroe arranged for her to buy a .22 rifle from a gun dealer but she was a bad shot and short tempered and was refused membership of the club. She did manage to buy a Webley .45 and a Smith & Wesson .38 from other members. During this time Brady had taken an interest in photography starting with a box brownie camera and soon upgrading as well as installing a dark room and lights. They took photos of each other some being sexually explicit.

Hindley recounts that Brady started to turn his thoughts to 'committing the perfect murder' in July 1963 after a drinking bout on German wine. He often spoke about the film 'Compulsion' where two men murder a 12 year old boy and get away with it because of their young age.

In 1963 Brady moved in with Hindley at her grandmother's house in Bannock Street and on 12th July they committed their first murder, Pauline Reade a friend of Hindley's younger sister Maureen was the victim. Reade had been in a short relationship with

David Smith, a local lad with criminal convictions who was questioned but released.

On the 12th July Brady had told Hindley that he was going to 'commit the perfect murder' that day. After work he told her to drive around the area whilst he followed on his motor bike. When he had selected a victim he would flash his headlight. The first time he flashed Hindley did not stop as she knew the girl as an 8 year old neighbour of her mothers. It was not until 7.30pm they stopped next to 16 year old Pauline Read who was on her way to a dance. Once Reade was in the van Hindley asked her to help her search for an expensive glove she had lost on Saddleworth Moor, Reade agreed and they drove there. When Brady arrived Hindley told Reade he had come to help and sent her off with Brady on some pretence that she would join them soon. Thirty minutes later Brady came back and took Hindley to where Reade lay dying with cuts to her throat. When Hindley asked if he had raped her he replied 'of course I did'. Brady then took a spade he had hidden on a previous visit and whilst Hindley went back to the van he buried

Reade on the moor. Brady's account of the murder differs from Hindleys. He says Hindley was present in the attack and participated in the sexual assault.The Police found nobody who had seen Reade before she disappeared.

On the evening of 23rd November 1963 12 year old John Kilbride was offered a lift home from a market in Ashton-under-Lyne by Brady and Hindley who said his parents might worry that he was out so late. They also promised him a bottle of sherry for his parents but said they would have to detour to their home to pick it up. On the way Brady suggested it wouldn't take a minute to have a quick search on the moor for an expensive glove Hindley had lost on there recently. At the moor Brady went off with Kilbride and sexually assaulted him before strangling him with string after failing to kill him with a six inch serrated knife. Police and volunteers undertook a search the next day, took 700 statements and printed 500 missing person posters. After 8 days 2000 volunteers scoured waste ground and derelict buildings in the area. Hindley is thought to have checked on the grave a week after the murder and again on 21st December 1963, each time hiring a vehicle.

In the evening of 16th June 1964 Hindley had 12 year old Keith Bennett help her load some boxes into a mini-van after which she said she would drive him home to his grandmother's house in Longsight, Manchester. Brady was in the back of the van and they drove to Saddleworth Moor, once again saying they were going to look for a lost glove. On the moor Hindley parked in a lay-by and Brady and Bennett went off to search for the non-existent glove. Brady returned 30 minutes later carrying a spade he had hidden there earlier and said he had sexually assaulted Bennett and strangled him with string.

On 26th December 1964 10 year old Lesley Ann Downey was alone at a fairground when Hindley and Brady approached near to her and deliberately dropped some shopping they were carrying on the ground. They had obviously planned this and asked Downey to help them pick it up and carry it to their car, and then into their home. At the house Downey was stripped, gagged and made to pose for photographs before being raped and killed, possibly by strangulation. Hindley said later that she had gone to run a bath for the girl and returned to find her dead. Brady claims Hindley killed her. The following morning they drove Downey's body to Saddleworth Moor and buried her with her clothes at her feet.

On the 6th October 1965 Brady planned another murder. He had Hindley drive him to Manchester Railway Station and left her in the car whilst he went to get a victim. He returned with Edward Evans a 17 year old apprentice engineer, it is not known whether the two knew each other previously or not but Evans was taken to Brady and Hindley's home at 16 Wardle Brook Avenue in Hattersley and they all started to drink. Brady had told Evans that Hindley was his sister and might be persuaded to have sex later on. During the evening Hindley went to fetch David Smith who was the husband of her younger sister Maureen. Smith was a nasty character with a string of criminal convictions including many with violence. Brady had formed a relationship with him and Smith had become very loyal to and somewhat in awe of Brady. When Hindley and Smith came to the house she told him to wait outside for a flashing light signal before knocking at the door. The lights flashed and Smith was let in by Brady who, according to Smiths evidence later, asked him 'if he was there to collect some wine bottles?' and left him in the kitchen. A short time later Smith says he heard screams from the living room and Hindley called for him to help Brady. In the room he found Brady standing over Evans with a small axe which he brought down on Evan's head and then strangled him with electric flex. They put Evan's body in a plastic sheet and took it up into the spare bedroom. Brady had twisted his ankle and couldn't walk properly let alone carry a body out to the car so it was agreed that Smith would return the next morning with a baby's pram to wheel the body to the car and then they would go to the moors and bury it. When he got home at 3am in the morning Smith was very sick and told Maureen what he had witnessed. As daylight broke he made his way to a public phone box and rang the police who picked him up from there and took him to Hyde police station where he gave a full account of what he had witnessed at Brady's.

Superintendent Robert Talbot and a Detective Sergeant went to Brady's and disguised themselves by wearing bread delivery men's overalls over their uniforms. They went to the back door of 16 Wardle Brook Avenue where Hindley denied her husband was at home or indeed that she even had a husband. When Talbot identified himself and showed her his warrant card she led them into the house where they found Brady on a sofa writing a letter to his employer saying he couldn't work because of his sprained ankle. Talbot told them he was investigating a violent episode that had been reported as happening in the house the previous evening and made a search of the house. The spare bedroom was locked and Hindley said the key was at her place of work. When Talbot said they'd take her to fetch it Brady realised it was all over and told her to open the room. After finding the gruesome contents Talbot arrested Brady on suspicion of murder. Brady told them that 'Eddie and I had an argument that got out of control.'

Hindley was not arrested but went to the police station with Brady. She refused to make a statement about Evan's death beyond saying it had been an awful accident. She was allowed to go back home on condition she checked in at the police station the next day. She went to her work place and asked to be dismissed so that she could claim unemployment benefit. At work she went through Brady's things and burnt an envelope which later she claimed she had not opened but that it contained their earlier bank robbery plans. On 11th October she too was arrested as an accessory to the murder of Edward Evans and remanded in custody at Risley Police Station.

Police uncovered an exercise book with John Kilbride's name in it during a search of 16 Wardle Brook Avenue which alerted them to suspect Brady and Hindley's involvement in other child kidnaps and possible murders. Brady insisted that he was helped in the murder of Evans by Smith and that Hindley had nothing to do with the actual killing. Smith now opened up about his friendship with Brady and told the police that Brady had asked Smith to return anything of his that might be 'incriminating' a few weeks before which included 'dodgy books'. Smith said they were put into small suitcases but they weren't in the house when the police searched it. Smith did say that Brady 'had a thing about railway stations' and the police made a search of the left luggage at Manchester stations and found them. The ticket was later found hidden in Hindley's prayer book. The cases contained costumes, books, notes, photographs and negatives including 9 pornographic photos of Lesley Ann Downey, naked and with a scarf across her mouth. An audio tape of a girl screaming and pleading for help was also found and identified as the voice of Lesley Ann Downey by her mother.

A neighbour of Brady and Hindley was 12 year old Pat Hodges who told police she had been with them to the Moor several times. She pointed out to the police their favourite places to stop and walk on the moor. Police immediately searched the area with dogs and on 16th October found Lesley Ann Downey's body and clothing. The clothing was identified by her mother.

The photographs in the recovered suitcases had a number of moors scenes amongst them which tied in with Smith telling the police that Brady had boasted of photographs that proved he had committed multiple murders. The police showed the photos to locals who were asked if they could identify the parts of the moor shown. On 21st October they uncovered the decomposed body of Kilbride which was identified by his clothing. That day Hindley and Brady, who were already being held for the murder of Evans, were charged with Downey's murder as well. Brady admitted to taking the photos of Downey but insisted she had been brought to the house by two men he had met before and taken away by them, alive, after he took the photos.

On 6th December there was the committal hearing. Brady was charged with the murders of Evans, Kilbride and Downey and Hindley with the murders of Evans and Downey and of harbouring Brady in the knowledge that he had killed Kilbride. The proceedings took eleven days after which the pair were committed for trial at Chester.

The trial began on 19th April 1966 before Justice Fenton Atkinson. Brady and Hindley were kept behind security screens as public anger against them was at fever pitch and attempts on their lives were not expected but had to be considered. The Attorney General, Sir Elwyn Jones led the prosecution together with William Marrs-Jones. Emlyn Hooson QC defended Brady and Godfrey Heilpern defended Hindley, both being experienced Queen's Counsel.

Both pleaded not guilty with Brady being on the stand for eight hours and Hindley for six. The jury was out for two hours and returned guilty verdicts on Brady for all three murders and on Hindley for the murder of Downey and Evans. Luckily for them the death penalty had been abolished while they were both in remand and the Judge gave them the harshest sentence he could which was three life terms to Brady and two to Hindley. Brady went to Durham Prison and Hindley to Holloway.

David Smith was used as the chief witness for the prosecution and sold his story to the News of the World for £1000

Over the following years Brady and Hindey made various confessions and suggestions to other inmates of more bodies being buried on the moor and the police made other searches on two occasions taking Brady with them but nothing was found. Brady told the BBC that he committed another five murders and listed them as a man in Manchester, another buried on Saddleworth Moor, a woman who he claimed he dropped into a canal and two others in Scotland. There was no evidence or connection on police files to substantiate these claims so no action was taken. Despite both Brady and Hindley confessing to the murders of Pauline Read and Keith Bennett the DPP decided not to prosecute them as they were already serving life sentences so no further punishment could be given.

Brady was moved from Ashworth Hospital to Durham prison after the trial and requested to be put into solitary confinement, which he was. After nineteen years he was sent to high security Ashworth Psychiatric Hospital after being diagnosed as a psychopath and given a full life tariff on his sentence. He had a regular fan club of mainly women with whom he corresponded and one even sent him paracetamol tablets hidden inside a book after he said he wanted to commit suicide. He even wrote a book called The Gates of Janus about serial killing and killers which found an underground publisher in the USA but public outrage prevented any UK publisher from taking it onboard. He wrote to the mother of the one undiscovered victim, Keith Bennett, telling her would take the police to the approximate place of burial but the offer was rejected as Brady trying to influence a parole board as he was now talking about being released, something that was never, ever on the cards. He applied to be taken out of psychiatric care and put back into prison but this was also refused. He had several 48 hour hunger strikes which caused the authorities to fit him with a feeding tube. He died 15th May 2017 of natural causes with the body being cremated and the ashes disposed of at sea during the night.

****

1967 FRED & ROSE WEST.

Fred West was a serial killer convicted of several murders and sexual assaults in the 1960s-70s. Together with his wife Rose they murdered and dismembered bodies of women and girls including two of their own family. Fred West was born in Much Marcle, Herefordshire, known as the home of Weston Cider Makers, on 29th September 1941 to Walter and Daisy West. They lived in a cottage on Moorcourt Farm, Much Marcle. 'He was always such a nice boy' his aunt told the press after he was convicted. One of six children Fred was his mother's favourite and rumours abounded in the village that an incestuous relationship had developed between them and between his father and the girls in the family, rumours that have never been substantiated. West dropped out of school and became a jobbing farm worker. He had a serious motorcycle accident at 17 and the head injuries necessitated a steel plate being inserted over the wound in his head. Doctors say this may have had an effect on his later behaviour. This wound was exacerbated when he fell off a fire escape at the local youth club in Ledbury and incurred further head injuries. His behaviour got pretty bad and he was pulled by the police many times for various thefts and small crimes. In 1961 the turning point came after he made a 13 year old girl who was a friend of the family pregnant and his parents decided they had had enough of him and kicked him out of the family home. He got a job in the construction industry as a labourer but was sacked for stealing and arrested again for rape and sex with a minor. At his trial for rape he escaped a custodial sentence after his defence argued it was the previous head trauma that caused his behaviour, but he was still convicted of child molestation. In 1962 West married (Rena) Bernadette Costello, a Scottish prostitute from Coatbridge Lanarkshire with a record for burglary who was already pregnant by an Asian bus driver at the time of their marriage. The child was born in March 1963 and they called her Charmaine. The family moved to Savoy Street, Bridgtown, Glasgow. West's liking for young girls grew when he took a job as an ice cream van driver which meant he met many young people to prey on. In 1964 Rena and Fred had a daughter, Anna Marie. At this time they also met Anna McFall who spent a lot of time at their flat after the death of her boyfriend in a workplace accident. Both Rena and Fred engaged in several affairs with different people during their marraige. On 4th November 1965 Fred accidentally ran his ice cream van over a small boy who died from his injuries. Afraid of reprisals from the locals he, Rose and McFall together with the children returned to Gloucester renting a caravan at Timberland Caravan Park in Bishop's Cleeve and Fred took work in a slaughter house. Some psychiatrists put this work as having created his interest, if not obsession, with death and dismemberment.

In Gloucester at the time there were eight reported incidents of sexual assault where the attacker's description fitted Fred but the link was not made. The marriage failed and Rena left for Scotland leaving the children with West and McFall. Times got worse and they ended up living in a small caravan. McFall became pregnant with West's child in 1967 and started to insist he divorce Rena and marry her so they could get enhanced benefit payments and apply for housing. Fred was unwilling to do so and killed the pregnant McFall in July 1967 burying her in a field between Much Marcle and Kempley after first cutting off her fingers and toes and then dismembering the body, something he continued to do in his future murders. Rena returned and moved into another caravan at Lake House Caravan Park with Fred. In January 1968 fifteen year old Mary Bastholm was taken from a bus stop in Gloucester and disappeared. West was linked to it but the circumstantial evidence was not strong enough to charge him. (See update at the end of this piece)

In November 1968 he had left Rena and met Rose Letts, who was to become his lifelong partner in murder. He saw her at Cheltenham bus station and pestered her for some time before she dated him and then moved in leaving her job as an assistant in a bread shop on the proviso that Fred would give her enough money each week to give her parents to maintain the lie that she was still working at the shop.

Rosemary 'Rose' Letts was born in Devon on November 29th 1953. Both parents suffered from mental illness and electro therapy for deep depression had been given to her mother during the pregnancy which doctors later diagnosed could have affected Rose's poor school marks and aggressive nature. She also had a weight problem as a teenager and developed a sexual interest in older men. Her parent's marriage broke up due to her father's violence and Rose left with her mother. She moved back in with her father after a short period at about the same time as she met and became intimate with Fred West who had left Rena, she was still in her teens. Her father didn't like Fred and even contacted social services about the relationship and threatened West personally. Nothing happened and Rose was soon pregnant with West's child and left home to look after West's two children by Rena Costello when West went to prison on various theft and fine evasion charges. Rose gave birth to daughter Heather in 1970. Rose was subject to violent outbursts and it is thought the pressure of three small children whilst being a near child herself caused Rose to snap and murder eight year old Charmaine in 1971. The truth is not really known but with Fred in jail at the time of Charmaine's disappearance conjecture has it that Rose hid the body in a coal bunker until Fred was released and then he removed the fingers and toes and they buried the body. This of course gave Fred a hold over Rose. When Rena got worried about no contact from her daughter and came looking she was strangled, extensively dismembered and put in plastic bags before being buried near to West's first victim Anna McFall in a field close to Yewtree Coppice at Letterbox Field near Much Marcle.

Fred and Rose secretly married in Gloucester in January 1972 and their second child, another girl called Mae was born in June that year at the same time as they moved into 25 Cromwell street, Gloucester, a house large enough for them, their family and to be able to take in lodgers to help pay the rent. He later bought the house from the Council for £7000 and converted the upper floors into bedsits to rent out to cover the mortgage. He installed a washroom and kitchen on the 1st floor and forbade his lodgers to come down to the ground floor where the West family lived other than to use the stairs and hall for entry and exit. The garden was for the West's use only. The mortgage and family income was further subsidised by Rose's earnings from prostitution. Fred designed a room for her to operate this business in and drilled peepholes so he could watch. A red warning light on the outside of the door warned the children that mum was busy and to keep out. Fred was by this time committing acts of bondage and sex on underage girls. Fred had Rose advertise her sexual services in a local contact magazine and encouraged her to have sex with the lodgers, male and female, plus men Fred brought home from his work. He particularly liked to see her with West Indian men. Fred would make up a threesome and many who participated remember how the pair liked to move into bondage and dominance scenarios with pain attached. His relationship with Bill Letts, Rose's father had mended and together they opened a cafe called the Green Lantern but it failed. When Letts learnt of his daughter's prostitution he visited and had sex with Rose whilst Fred observed them through the peep holes. Fred made his cellar at Cromwell Street into a torture chamber and assaulted his own daughter Anna Marie there. She was subjected to brutal rape as Rose held her down. It was a regular obscenity with the child threatened with severe beatings if she mentioned it to anybody. When she was thirteen Anna Marie was offered for sex to Rose's clients, they being told she was sixteen. They extended their behaviour outside the family by hiring seventeen year old Caroline Owens as a nanny and imprisoning her in the cellar where she was kept naked and suffered many rapes by Fred after trying to leave the family. Miraculously she escaped and reported the occurrences to the police. Charges were laid but West convinced a Magistrates Court that Owens had consented to the acts. They escaped with fines. Rose was again pregnant at the time with their first son, Stephen, born that August.

Over the next years Lynda Gough, Lucy Partington, Juanita Mott, Therese Siegenthaler,

Alison Chamber, Shirley Robinson and fifteen year old schoolgirls Carol Ann Cooper and Shirley Hubbard were brutally sexually attacked, murdered, dismembered and buried under the cellar floor by the Wests.

Lynda Gough, 19 would visit a male lodger at 25 Cromwell street and had affairs with two lodgers and moved in with the Wests in 1973. When she disappeared the Wests told her mother that she had been asked to leave after she had hit one of the children. Carol Ann Cooper was 19 and abducted from a bus stop in Worcester taken to the house and suspended from a beam in the cellar ceiling whilst being abused and murdered before being dismembered and buried there. Four further victims were to suffer the same treatment. After killing Jaunita Mott in April 1975 Fred concreted over the entire cellar floor. This later became the children's play room. Shirley Robinson was an 18 year old lodger who was pregnant when killed in1978. Rose may have thought the child was Fred's and was also pregnant herself at the time. Shirley was buried in the garden. Later pathology showed the unborn child had been cut from the body. A month after the killing Robinson Rose submitted a form for maternity grant money on Robinson's behalf to Gloucester Council. Anybody asking after Robinson was told she had gone to live with her father in West Germany. The last known murder by the Wests with a sexual motive was that of Alison Chambers in 1979. She had absconded from a children's home and became their live-in nanny. She was also buried in the garden. Rose sent a letter written by Chambers to her mother before being killed from a post box in Northampton and told people Chambers had gone there to a new job.

Rose had more children, not all thought to be fathered by Fred, eight in all by 1983 and those that were darker skinned were told by Fred that they had a West Indian grandmother. Louise was born in 1978, Barry in 1980, Rosemary in 1982 and Lucyanna in 1983. All were aware as they got older of the activities in the cellar but Fred ruled with an iron fist and fear kept them quiet. Between 1972 and

92 the West children were admitted to the A&E departments of local hospitals thirty one times with injuries reported as accidents by the Wests and never reported further to Social Services. Fred's interest in incest accelerated when Anna Marie moved out to live with her boyfriend and his attention turned to Heather and Mae. Heather resisted and in 1987 confided in a friend what was going on in the cellar. The Wests found out that she had spoken about it and murdered and dismembered her before burying her in the back garden at number 25, son Stephen helped dig the hole without realising what it was for.

The number of sex acts on underage girls was growing all the time and not every one resulted in murder so rumours were beginning to reach the ear of the police. In August 1992 DC Hazel Savage led a search of 25 Cromwell Street and found child pornography and clear evidence of real child abuse having occurred in the house. West was arrested for rape and sodomy of a minor and Rose arrested for assisting in the rape of a minor. After agreeing to testify against their parents the children recanted and would not and were sent into foster care. The police continued to look for Heather and heard the 'family joke' about her being under the patio so many times that they decided to excavate the garden. On being told this and shown a warrant allowing it Rose became distraught and abusive and had Stephen phone Fred who was at work and get him home. Fred came quickly and assured the officers that Heather had left and was with a drugs ring in Gloucester. The police did not believe him and put a uniformed guard on the garden over night before digging in the morning. In the morning Fred told Stephen to look after Rose as 'I've done something really bad', and for him to 'sell the story to a paper for as much money as you can get.' He then formally admitted to the police that he had strangled Heather in a fit of rage. He even offered to point out the part of the garden she was buried under. Heather's dismembered body was excavated plus a further thigh bone. When questioned Fred admitted there were a further two bodies under the garden. The police put Rose in a safe house in Dursley and obtained a warrant to search the complete house and land. Fred knew what they would find and during an interview passed a note to his solicitor which read, 'I Frederick west, authorise my solicitor, Howard Ogden, to advise Superintendent Bennett (who was leading the murder investigation) that I wish to admit a further nine killings, expressly Charmaine, Rena, Lynda Gough and others to be identified. Signed F.West'. When questioned about this note and his claims Fred explained there were five in the cellar floor and one beneath the ground floor bathroom. He was taken back to 25 Cromwell street and indicated precisely where the bodies were. The bodies were found and exhumed but some bones were missing which Fred refused to explain. Fred insisted that Rose had nothing to do with the murders but the police didn't believe him and arrested her on 20th April 1994 on offences of rape of an eleven year old girl and physical assault on an eight year old boy dating back to 1970s. She was refused bail and remanded in maximum security at Pucklechurch Prison where she was intensively questioned about the murders. On

25th April she was charged with Lynda Gough's murder. On 6th May they were both charged with five counts of murder. As well as the Cromwell Street murders Fred confessed to those of his first wife and step-daughter and to the burial place of Anne McFall's body. With his guidance the remains were unearthed between April and June. He was transferred to HM Prison Birmingham and put on suicide watch. Fred West was charged with twelve counts of murder and Rose with nine. At the Magistrates court at Gloucester Rose spurned his attempts to place a hand on her shoulder. The strict suicide watch had been relaxed and then before the trial he hanged himself with knotted bed sheets in Birmingham Prison on January 1st 1995.

Unlike Fred, Rose did not confess and played the victim part telling the police that she had been afraid of what her husband would do to her if she hadn't helped him. She was found guilty of ten murders and sentenced to life imprisonment. She is currently in HM Prison New Hall where rumour has it she was in a lesbian relationship with Myra Hindley who died in 2002.

Police firmly believe the Wests were responsible for many unsolved murders and disappearances. They estimate the Wests committed ten murders between 1971 and 1979, at least seven of which were for sexual purposes. After the rash of murders between 1973 and 1975, they are not known to have committed any more murders until 1978. They committed one further murder in 1979, then nothing until they murdered their daughter in 1987. Police do not know of any further murders they committed before their 1994 arrest.

During formal questioning, Fred confessed to murdering up to thirty people, indicating that there are up to eighteen other undiscovered victims.

Fred's body was cremated in Coventry on March 29th 1995. The service was held with just the four family members present. No hymns were sung. His ashes were scattered at the Welsh holiday resort of Barry Island, a place he had often visited as a child and with his family for holidays.

After their parents arrest in 1994 the surviving four youngest West children were given new identities to protect them from the public anger against their family and each remained in foster care until deemed suitable to go their own ways.

The remains of Rena and her daughter Charmaine were cremated in Kettering and at Anna Marie West's insistence mother and daughter shared the same coffin. It was made clear that no 'roses' were to be sent or brought to the service by any mourners.

DC Hazel savage whose tenacity in investigating and prosecuting the Wests was awarded the MBE.

Fred's younger brother John hanged himself in the garage at his Gloucester home in November 1996. At the time of his suicide he was waiting for the jury's verdict in his own trial for alleged multiple rapes of his niece Anna Marie at Cromwell Street in the 1970s.

In March 1996 Rose West appealed her sentence contending that the press coverage had influenced and made witness testimony unreliable and that no physical evidence existed that proved she had taken part in any of the murders. The appeal failed. In July 1997 the Home Secretary Jack Straw added a whole life tariff to her sentence.

Both of Rose West's biological children and her stepdaughter Anna Marie visited her regularly in prison although she stopped seeing them once Mae questioned her culpability in the murders. It is rumoured that Anne Marie who changed her name from Anna to Anne does still visit.

The body of Fred's former best friend Terence Crick was found in his car in the Scarborough district of Hackness in January 1996. He was forty-eight and first became acquainted with Fred whilst he lived at the Lake House Caravan Park in 1969. Crick had reported Fred to the police several times after Fred showed him surgical instruments that Fred said he used to perform illegal abortions. Crick had also maintained that Fred had asked him to keep a look out for young pregnant girls who might be interested in an abortion. The fact that his information given to the police had not been acted upon apparently played on his mind and led him to suicide by carbon monoxide poisoning.

The West's house in Cromwell Street was demolished in October 1996 with every piece of the debris destroyed or taken to landfill sites to discourage souvenir hunters. The site was later made into a public pathway.

In 1999 Anne Marie West attempted to drown herself in the River Severn but passers by pulled her out. Stephen West is also known to have made an unsuccessful suicide attempt in 2002 by hanging himself. In 2004 he was jailed for nine months under a pseudonym for having illegal sex with a fourteen year old girl on multiple occasions. The youngest son, Barry, took a drug overdose that killed him in October 2020 at the age of 40.

Update May 2021. An independent television production company filming a documentary on the Wests in Gloucester did some ground sonar research at the Clean Plate Cafe in Southgate Street. The cafe under another the name

The Pop In Cafe' was known as a regular place that Fred West visited about the time of 15 year old Mary Bastholm's disappearance in 1968. Mary worked there and Fred was doing building work in the cellar at the time. The TV company alerted the police that their ground sonar had found voids beneath the concrete floor and behind the walls. At the time of writing the police have moved in and are excavating the cellar.

****

1971 MALCOLM GREEN

On 21st June 1971 in Cardiff, Malcolm Green bumped into prostitute Glenys Johnson 41 and killed her on waste ground near the docks. He slashed her throat with a broken bottle and then phoned the police and said 'Have you found the body? There will be four more. This is the Ripper'

The call was traced to British Steel's East Moors works where Green was employed. He had made the call after the murder when he decided to go to the works, shower and clean his bloody clothes.

On receipt of the phone call the police instituted a search of the area and found Johnson's body stuffed under a car on the waste ground off Wharf Street. Her head had nearly been decapitated by the glass and the rest of her body cut into with deep slashes. Green was soon arrested and confessed to the murder but later accused the police of making up a false statement on his behalf. When they visited his home, a flat on the Coed-Y-Gores estate in Llanederyn where he lived with his wife, they found a dummy made from a rolled carpet dressed in a shirt and coat with a knife stuck in where the chest would be and red paint daubed around it.

Green was sentenced to life at Cardiff Assizes with 25years minimum term for Johnson's murder on November 5th 1971.

He was released from Leyhill open prison in Bristol in October 1989 having served 18 years and deemed safe to release by the prison psychiatrists. He stayed in Bristol and made friends with Clive Tully, a young tourist from New Zealand who was touring around the world getting work where he could to finance the trip. On 19th March 1990 Green murdered Tully with a hammer and cut the body up into quite small bits which he then put into bags that he took over the Severn Bridge into Wales and left at various places along rural back roads. This act was seized on by the media who named the case 'The Body in the Bags Killings'. The first bags were found on 22nd March 1990 by a school teacher in a lay-by on the A467 near Rogerstone, Newport. Inside two holdalls were dismembered upper arms, legs and a torso, each part individually wrapped in plastic and taped. Four days later on 26th March a farmer at St Brides, Wentloog found a head in a red plastic bag and two hands nearby in a white plastic bag. The remains were identified as Tulley's after a police graphic artist produced a computer enhanced photo fit of the victim, Tulley's friendship with Green was known to neighbours who called the police and when they went to the flat Tulley was staying at they found blood stains with Green's fingerprints in them. Green's fingerprints were also on most of the bags. Green was arrested on 30th March 1990 at his girlfriend's house in Fishponds, Bristol. He denied the murder although his friendship with Tulley was admitted. In November 1991 he was found guilty by a jury and sentenced to Life Imprisonment shouting his innocence as he was taken down. The Home Secretary added a 'full life' tariff to his sentence. It became known that Green could have been mentally scarred aged 20 when his elder brother was decapitated by a train whilst going to a football match in Reading and Green had the task of identifying the mutilated body in the morgue.

****

1973 PETER GEORGE DINSDALE known as 'Bruce Lee.'

Dinsdale, who later changed his name to that of his favourite Kug Fu actor, Bruce Lee, was born in Manchester on July 31st 1960. He was the son of a sex worker and from birth had epilepsy, partial paralysis and a deformed arm. He spent the first three years of his life living with his grandmother before moving in with his mother and her partner until that relationship ended and he was taken into care by the council and sent into various children's homes where he later admitted he took part in homosexual practices with the staff and other boys. He was not well educated and when he passed sixteen went to work as a labourer.

On December 4th 1979 a fire in a residential house in Hull, East Yorkshire killed three young brothers Charles 15, Peter 12 and Paul Hastie 8. The police were called in after the fire officers noticed paraffin on the floor of the front porch. An incident room was set up and investigations started with the police noticing an indifferent attitude to the boy's deaths from the neighbours. Apparently the family were a 'problem' family of thieves and troublemakers. The father was in prison at the time of the fire. The police began looking for an arsonist with a grudge against the Hastie family who may have taken revenge by torching the house. They were amazed when they started to interview local people and came to Lee's turn. He readily admitted in great detail to pouring paraffin through the letter box and igniting it as a revenge on Charles Hastie with whom he was having a homosexual relationship and of being spurned by Angeleena Hastie who he had a crush on. Lee told police Hastie had threatened to go to the police unless Lee gave him money on a regular basis and report their relationship and being a minor Lee would then be sent back to youth custody which he wanted to avoid at any cost. Further questioning about Lee's life revealed his love of starting fires and that he was a pyromaniac and had started nine other fatal fires in Hull over the past seven years. None of those fires had been thought suspicious at the time with inquest verdicts of misadventure being recorded for each. Arson was never considered. A total of twenty six people had perished in those fires from a six-month-old baby, through a young mother and her three sons to eleven elderly men in Wensley Lodge, a care home. Countless more were injured whilst escaping. Of all the fires he started only three were against people where Lee went looking for personal revenge. Lee was driven around the city of Hull and pointed out the various houses he said he had set fire to, he couldn't always remember the date of the arson but records later confirmed his identifications. The police were still amazed and set a test by taking him to a house where a fire had occurred and a criminal conviction for arson had already been made. Lee stated he had never been near the area. The police were then convinced he was telling the truth about the other blazes he laid claim too. Lee showed no remorse for the deaths and said he just liked fire and had never even thought about the occupants of the houses, he was a true pyromaniac.

On 20th June 1981 at Leeds Crown court Lee pleaded not guilty to twenty six counts of murder but guilty to twenty six counts of manslaughter on the grounds of diminished responsibility and to eleven counts of arson. Lee was sent to Park Lane Special Hospital in Liverpool and later transferred to Rampton Secure Hospital. The trial rated second in importance in the media as the trial of Peter Sutcliffe was happening at the same time and Lee was charged with manslaughter not murder. In 1983 a public enquiry dismissed Lee's claim to have started the Wensley Lodge fire after further forensic evidence was given to show it was the result of an accident As a result the eleven manslaughter convictions were quashed on appeal.

At the time of the trial in 1981 sections of the local and national press were beginning to cast doubt on Lee's guilt. They noted that Lee's physical handicap would probably have made it nigh on impossible for him to break windows and climb inside houses to start fires. They also asked questions as to how a boy with Lee's low intelligence would cover his escape routes in the thoughtful way the police had suggested he had. They also suggested that the Hastie fire was quite likely a gangland revenge against the husband who was known to have several enemies in the criminal underworld. The dismissal of Lee's part in the Wensly Care Home fire was mainly based on the Times account of Lee's known movements that night that placed him well away from the scene and they argued that with a deformed hand it was unlikely that Lee rode a bike 3 miles to the Home carrying a large can of paraffin and very unlikely that nobody would have seen him on the road.

At the time of writing Lee is still a secure mental institution.

****

1974 PATRICK MACKAY

Patrick Mackay was born in Dartford on 25th September 1952 to Harold Mackay and his wife Marion, a mixed race woman who he had met in Guyana. Harold Mackay was an alcoholic subject to bouts of physical abuse against his son Patrick. In 1962 Mackay's father died of a heart attack. Mackay at just ten years old refused to accept his father's death, refused to attend the funeral in Scotland and took on the mantel of 'head of the family' carrying on his father's violence against his mother and two sisters. The family moved to Gravesend where the domestic unrest carried on with regular visits from the police. Mackay was sent to various specialist schools and institutions eighteen times before his 22nd birthday with both his psychiatrists and the police growing more and more concerned at his increasing violent streak, tantrums and anger. He bullied younger children and stole from them, from elderly ladies houses and people in the street using violence. An arsonist side to his character surfaced when he set fire to a local church. At just fifteen his psychiatrist offered an opinion that 'Mackay had all the signs of growing into being a cold, psychopathic killer'. This diagnosis of Mackay being a psychopath led to Mackay's internment at Moss Side Hospital in 1968. He was released in 1972.

On release Mackay moved to London and became obsessed with Nazism calling himself 'Franklin Bollvolt the 1st' and collecting Nazi paraphernalia that filled his small flat. He took to drink and drugs and was befriended by a local priest, Father Anthony Crean, near his mother's home in Kent which he visited often to steal or borrow money. He even broke into Crean's home and stole a cheque for £30. He was arrested, prosecuted and ordered to repay the amount which he never did. He returned to London and then on 21st March 1975, aged twenty two, Mackay went to Crean's home in the village of Shorne and hacked the priest to death with an axe. Knowing Mackay's past history with Father Crean he was quickly made chief suspect and arrested. Under interrogation Mackay claimed to have murdered eleven people over the previous two years, mostly elderly woman who he said he had stabbed or strangled whilst robbing them. The evidence was poor on most of his claims but he was charged with five murders, two were later dropped through lack of hard evidence and in November 1975 the murder charges were reduced to manslaughter due to his diminished responsibility and he was sentenced to life imprisonment with a whole life tariff.

Mackay was considered for release in 2020 but at the time of writing this has been postponed as fresh cold case investigations with new forensic science that was unavailable in the 70s are taking place into the murders he claimed.

****

1974 ROBERT MAUDSLEY

A very strange case indeed. Robert John Maudsley murdered four people, three of them whilst inside prison serving a life sentence for the first one. His nickname was Hannibal The Cannibal after it was alleged that he ate part of the brain of one of the prison victims.

One of twelve children from Speke in Liverpool he was cared for in an orphanage from an early age in Crosby and then taken back by his parents aged eight and then later on removed from them again by Social Services. In the late 1960s he moved to London and worked as a sex worker to fund his drug addiction. He was given psychiatric help after several suicide attempts and claimed he was hearing voices in his head from an early age telling him to kill his parents. He was later to state that if he had killed them he wouldn't have gone on to kill the others.

In 1974 Maudsley was picked up by John Farrell aged 30 in Wood Green, London for sex and Farrell showed him pictures of children he claimed to have abused sexually. Maudsley garrotted Farrell and surrendered himself to the police asking for more psychiatric care as he felt he would repeat the action if he was not securely housed. He was found unfit to stand trial and was sent to Broadmoor. In 1977 he and David Cheeseman another patient took a third patient David Francis, a child molester, prisoner and locked themselves inside a cell. They tortured Francis for nine hours eventually killing him. Maudsley was sent to trial and convicted of manslaughter and sent to Wakefield prison for life imprisonment with a recommendation that he never be released.

In 1978 Maudsley murdered two fellow prisoners in Wakefield prison on the same day. He killed Salney Darwood 46, who was serving life for the murder of his wife by garrotting him and stabbing him in his cell, hiding the body under his bed. He then tried to get other prisoners to come into his cell but all refused so he went on the hunt for another victim eventually stabbing prisoner Bill Roberts 56, to death. He attacked Roberts dead skull with a self made knife and then banged it several times against a brick wall before calmly walking into the prison officer's room on the wing and telling him that they would be two short at the next roll call.

Maudsley was listed as too dangerous to be with other prisoners and was escorted by a minimum of four officers at all times when out of his cell. The prison authorities had a two-cell unit built in the basement for him 5.5 by 4.5 metres with large bulletproof spy windows through which he could be watched at all times. The lavatory and sink were bolted to the floor and the table and chair made of pressed cardboard. The bed was a concrete slab. A solid steel door allowed access to a small cage inside the cell perimeter made of thick acrylic panels with a small open slot at the base where food and drink was passed through. He was allowed out for one hour daily to exercise in the yard accompanied by six officers. No contact with other inmates was allowed. In 2000 he asked for a relaxation of the solitary terms, a cyanide capsule and a pet budgie, all were denied.

It has been established that Maudsley has a genius equivalent IQ, has asked to take an Open University degree course (refused), loves classical music, poetry and art. What turned him into a serial killer? His brother has said he believes it was the severe beatings their father gave them as children. Who knows?

****

1974 JOHN CHILDS

This is another peculiar case. John Childs, also known as Bruce Childs was a petty criminal who worked his way up into being a hit man for gangsters taking contract killings for money. He had at least six victims, maybe many more, but none, yes none, of the bodies have been found. He served for a short time in the army being dismissed for burglary. His wife divorced him in 1982 after his convictions.

After being arrested in 1978 for a series of bank robberies he was held at Waltham Abbey police station Essex where he told DCS Frank Cater out of the blue that he was fed up with his way of life and confessed to committing murders. After investigations took place on the evidence he provided he was charged and convicted of six murders, Terence Eve, Robert Brown, George Brett, Terry Brett, Frederick Sherwood and Ronald Andrews all killed between November 1974 and October 1978. No bodies or human remains were found and no murder weapons retrieved. He was tried at the Old Bailey and sentenced to six life sentences to be served concurrently. He then turned Queen's Evidence and accused his former employers Terry Pinfold and Harry MacKenney of being implicated in the murders. All had prison records. Childs said that Terence Eve who shared a business premises with Pinfold and MacKenny was killed so they could take over his business, his body was cut up and burnt. Childs said Andrews was killed because MacKenny was having an affair with Child's wife. Brett was shot with his ten year old son when they were lured to the premises on the pretence of being offered work. Sherwood owed them £7000 and was killed because he wouldn't pay it off and Brown was killed because he knew about Eve's murder and had a loose mouth. The defence counsel for Pinfold and MacKenny called two prisoners who were inside with Childs as witnesses as Childs had told them that he made up that MacKenny and Pinfold were involved. Both were found guilty of murder and convicted to life imprisonment, after several appeals they had their convictions overturned at the Court of Appeal in 2003. An interesting addition to this awful story was made by Child's wife Eileen in 2001 when she said in her autobiography that Child's name was false and he was really called Martin Jones and had taken the name Childs from a previous tenant of his flat. Why? She doesn't say. The mystery of the missing murders may have been cleared up in 1997 when Childs wrote to a pen friend (killers seem to attract pen friends, mainly female ones) that he had dismembered the victims' bodies at his council flat in Poplar and burnt them in the fireplace. In 1998 he held an interview with the Daily Mirror and confessed to five more murders. The police didn't take it seriously.

****

1974 TREVOR HARDY

'The Beast of Manchester'

In 1972 Trevor Joseph Hardy was jailed for five years for attacking and wounding a man with a pick-axe handle. He was released from Albany Jail, Isle of Wight on 18th November 1974. On New Years Eve, 31st December the same year 1974, just 43 days later he murdered Janet Lesley Stewart aged fifteen and buried her in a shallow grave on Newton Heath, North Manchester. She had been stabbed to death.

Whilst incarcerated Hardy was fixated by getting revenge on two people, Stanley O'Brien who had been his best friend and who he suspected of double crossing him and helping the police and fourteen year old Beverley Driver who had been his girlfriend but had found a boy of her own age whilst Hardy was in prison. She had written to him saying her family had forbade her to have anything to do with him. He told police he just wanted to kill them both. But when he was released from Albany in 1974 O'Brien had died. At Beverley Driver's home he threw an axe through a window. Running from there he spotted his first victim, Lesley Stewart. He stabbed her in the throat and buried her in a nearby clay quarry and returned over a number of weeks to cut up her body and bury the parts in other places. He threw her head into a lake. Lesley was listed as a missing person and it wasn't until later that police realised hardy had murdered her.

On July 15th 1975 Wanda Skala aged seventeen was walking home along Lightbowne Road, Moston, Manchester, from her work in a local hotel bar when she was hit with a broken piece of paving stone and dragged to a local building site where she was sexually assaulted and had one nipple bitten off and then murdered. Her naked body was found in a shallow grave on the site. Hardy was arrested for Skala's murder after bragging about it to his younger brother who informed the police. Sheilagh Farrow, his partner gave him an alibi and also secretly passed him a small file whilst in detention so he could file his teeth so they wouldn't match the bite marks on Skala's body. He was freed on the basis of Farrow's alibi.

He killed Mosoph six months later. On the 12th March 1976 Sharon Mosoph aged seventeen was murdered and thrown into the Rochdale Canal at Failsworth, Oldham. Hardy had been attempting to rob a local shopping centre that night and Mosoph had seen him whilst walking home from a work party. She had been strangled with her own tights, stripped naked, mutilated and had one of her nipples bitten off.

Police finally got him after he attacked 21 year old Christine Campbell who managed to get away and gave police a vital description and evidence. Hardy had gone into hiding but was found after plain clothes police followed Shelagh Farrow to a house in Stockport.

He was again arrested in August 1976 this time for the murders of both Skala and Mosoph. Whilst in detention he surprised the police by confessing to Janet Stewart's murder. She was listed only as a missing person at that time. He said he mistook Stewart for a schoolgirl with whom he was infatuated at the time. He took her ring and gave it to another girl as a token of his love for her. He also kept Skala's blood stained clothes and handbag for some reason.

At his trial he sacked his defence counsel and tried have the charges reduced to manslaughter. This was refused and he was found guilty of murder and sentenced to 3 life sentences with a minimum 30 year tariff. This was increased later by the Home Secretary to a 'whole life' tariff.

Neighbours in Manchester suspected that Hardy had killed others including seventeen year old Dorothy Leyden. Her family petitioned for a cold case review but the forensic DNA evidence exonerated Hardy.

On 23rd September 2012 Hardy suffered a heart attack in his cell in Wakefield prison and died in the prison hospital two days later. He had been in prison for thirty five years. The end of Hardy's murder spree coincided with the beginning of Peter Sutcliffe's 'The Yorkshire Ripper' and was somewhat knocked off the front pages by that turn of events.

****

1975 PETER SUTCLIFFE

Sutcliffe terrorised the north of England in the years 1975-80 and was nicknamed the Yorkshire Ripper. He murdered at least 13 times plus making many assaults on women in that time period as well.

He was born on June 2nd 1946 in Bingley to John and Kathleen Sutcliffe and was the eldest of six children. He left school at fifteen with no qualifications and took various jobs including at a mill and in factories. He also became a grave digger in 1964 and moved to a job in a local morgue where he took pride in showing friends jewellery he had stolen off bodies. In 1976 he took a job as a truck driver with T & W H Clark Ltd in Bradford and continued in that job throughout his killing spree.

His first known victim was 28 year old Wilma McCann who worked as a prostitute. He killed her in October 1975. In January 1976 he killed another sex worker, Emily Jackson forty-two. In 1977 he murdered four women. Irene Richardson age twenty-eight in February, Patricia Atkinson thirty-two in April, Jayne MacDonald sixteen in June and Jean

Jordan twenty-one in October. All were sex workers except MacDonald. Sutcliffe later told a psychiatrist that in order to justify the killings to himself he purposely developed a hatred of prostitutes. It emerged that as a young man he had been conned out of money by a prostitute and her pimp. He went on to kill three more in 1978, Yvonne Pearson twenty-two and Helen Rytka eighteen in January and then Vera Millward forty in May. All were sex workers. By this time the media had labelled him The Yorkshire Ripper and denouncing the police who seemed to be stumbling about and getting nowhere in identifying the killer. In 1979 he murdered Josephine Whittaker a nineteen year old bank employee seen as a 'respectable' woman who abducted and killed on her way home. As one detective put it, 'after that murder mass hysteria gripped the county as it seemed no woman was safe.' The murder of twenty year old Barbara Leach a student in September heightened this fear. In 1980 he killed Marguerite Walls a forty-seven year old civil servant in August and twenty year old Jacqueline Hill, a student in that November.

The police got lucky when he was seen by a patrol car sitting in a car with false number plates in the driveway of Light Trades House, Melbourne Avenue, Sheffield with a sex worker Olivia Reivers and was taken into custody. She must have been the luckiest woman in the world that night!! In the boot of the car police discovered screwdrivers and they became suspicious and went back to the place where they had arrested him in the car and searched it as at the time of his arrest he had been given a minute to go and relieve himself, they found a hammer and a knife thrown into some bushes. When interrogated he confessed to being the Yorkshire Ripper.

He was convicted in 1981 of the murder of thirteen women between 1975 and 1980 using a hammer, knife and sharpened screwdriver. He was also found guilty of attacking seven other women who survived. The Judge sentenced him to 20 life terms with a minimum of 30 years. The death penalty had been abolished in 1965 so was not available.

Investigators had missed several opportunities to stop Sutcliffe. They interviewed him nine times before his arrest and at one of these he was wearing the boots they had prints of at a murder scene but nobody noticed. A £5 note on the body of one of the sex worker victims was traced back to Sutcliffe's employer but an alibi that he was at a party that night had been accepted.

A hoax audio tape was sent by 'Wearside Jack' and police put a lot of manpower into tracing it and made themselves look very silly by the time it had been denounced. They also dismissed the claims of some women who were not sex workers which meant that the testimony from Marcella Claxton who was not a sex worker and survived Sutcliffe's attempt to kill her, was dismissed as was the sketch she made which was very accurate. It was not until Sutcliffe's death in 2020 that the police apologised for their 'mistakes, tone and terminology used by senior officers at the time.'

THE CHRONOLOGICAL DETAIL ...

1969 Sutcliffe's first victim was a sex worker who he met whilst looking for another sex worker who had tricked him out of money. He was with a friend Trevor Birdsall although Birdsall wasn't with him when he did the attack with a rock inside a sock. The woman had noted Birdsall's van number plate and the police caught up with Sutcliffe who admitted the assault but swore he had only used his fist. The woman did not press charges and the police told Sutcliffe he was very lucky she didn't as her husband was a nasty individual in jail for assault.

1975 Sutcliffe's 2nd assault was on the 5th July in Keighley where he attacked Anna Roguiskyj who was walking alone, knocking her unconscious with a hammer and then slashing her stomach with a knife. He was disturbed and fled the scene. Roguiskyj survived after surgery at Leeds General Infirmary but was traumatised by the attack. On the 5th August he attacked Olive Smelt in Halifax talking nicely to her before hitting her from behind with a hammer. He then opened her clothing and slashed her lower back with a knife. Lucky for Olive he was again disturbed and fled. She was traumatised but was able to tell the police that her attacker had a Yorkshire accent, this vital information was ignored so was the fact that both Keighley and Halifax did not have red light areas. On 27th August he attacked fourteen year old Tracy Browne in Silsden from behind, hitting her on the head five times in a country lane. He ran off when a car approached. Tracy needed brain surgery and Sutcliffe was never convicted for this attack but confessed to it in1992. His first murder was Wilma McCann on 30th October who he struck on the back of the head twice with a hammer, stabbed her in the throat and below her breasts five times and nine times around her belly button. West Yorkshire police employed 150 officers on the case and conducted 11,000 interviews but failed to find a culprit. In 2007 Wilma's daughter committed suicide after years of depression brought about by her mother's murder.

1976. Sutcliffe's next murder was in Leeds in January when he stabbed Emily Jackson forty-two a total of 52 times. Having financial worries Jackson had been persuaded to take on prostitution by her husband using the van the family roofing business owned. Sutcliffe picked her up outside the Gaiety Pub in Roundhay Road and took her to derelict buildings in the Manor Industrial Estate where he hit her on the head with a hammer and stabbed her with a sharpened screwdriver in the neck, chest and stomach. He stamped on her thigh which left a good imprint of his boot, the same boot he wore when being interviewed a few days later and not noted by the police at the time. Next he attacked Marcella Claxton in Roundhay Park, Leeds on 9th May after giving her a lift as she walked home from a party. He hit her from behind when they stopped for her to relieve herself, she was 4 months pregnant. She somehow survived and miscarried the pregnancy. She testified against him at his trial after undergoing intensive brain surgery and suffering chronic depression.

1977. Irene Richardson was attacked on February 5th in Roundhay Park. She was bludgeoned to death with a hammer and then her corpse mutilated with a knife. Tyre tracks nearby led to a long list of possible vehicles being involved. On 23rd April Sutcliffe murdered Patricia Atkinson a prostitute from Bradford in her flat. Boot prints were found on her bedclothes but not tied to those found on Emily Jackson's body. On 26th June he murdered sixteen year old Jayne McDonald in Chapeltown, she was not a sex worker and this gave added fear to women who had until then believed 'the Ripper' was only killing prostitutes. In July Sutcliffe seriously assaulted Maureen Long in Bradford, his attack was disturbed and he fled. She was in hospital for nine weeks. In October 1977 he killed prostitute Jean Jordan and remembered afterwards that he had given her a £5 note from his wages which was traceable. He had a party at his new home and afterwards went back to the body but couldn't find the note so mutilated the body and moved it. Her body was found on 9th October by the actor Bruce Jones (Les Battersby in Coronation Street) on land adjoining his allotment. The £5 note hidden in a secret compartment in Jordan's handbag was traced back through the bank to many companies including Sutcliffe's employer but his alibi of being at a family party held fast. On December 14th he attacked Marilyn Moore who survived and gave a good description of Sutcliffe to the police. Similar tyre tracks to those found at the scene of Irene Richardson's murder were found. Moore gave a good photo-fit of Sutcliffe and a good description of his car which had often been seen in red light districts but the police failed to catch him even after interviewing him for this assault.

1978. In January he killed again. Yvonne Pearson a twenty-one year old prostitute from Bradford was hit about the head and then had her chest jumped on several times and horse hair from a discarded sofa nearby stuffed into her mouth. Sutcliffe hid her body near Lumb Lane. Just ten days afterwards he killed eighteen year old Helen Rytka in Huddersfield hitting her on the head five times as she left his vehicle. He stripped most of her clothes off and stabbed her chest repeatedly. Her body was found underneath railway arches three days later. On 16th May he killed Vera Millward in The Manchester Royal Infirmary car park.

1979. Josephine Whitaker was his next victim on 4th April 1979. She was a nineteen year old clerk who he attacked on Saville Park Moor in Halifax as she walked home from work. At this time a lot of police resources were diverted to find the source of the fake audio tape messages from 'Wearside Jack' purporting to be the Ripper and goading the Assistant Chief Constable of West Yorkshire Police, George Oldfield who was the OIC of the operation. The hoaxer sent two letters to the police and the Daily Mirror in March 1978 boasting of his crimes and claiming responsibility for the killing of Joan Harrison in Preston in November 1975. A murder that the squad thought had not been released to the public and that gave 'Wearside Jack' some credence. Unknown to the murder squad the Harrison murder had been put into the public domain. Later in 2011 with DNA evidence Harrison's murderer was found to be sex offender Christopher Smith who had died in 2008. The 'Hoaxer' case was re-opened in 2005 after the advent of DNA profiling and samples taken from the letters and tape led to Samuel Humble, unemployed alcoholic resident on the Ford Estate in Sunderland whose DNA had been added to the data base after a drunk and disorderly offence in 2001. He was arrested, charged and convicted of attempting to pervert the course of justice and sentenced to eight years in 2006. He died 30th July 2019 aged sixty three. On 1st September Sutcliffe murdered Barbara Leach, twenty, a University Student in Bradford and dumped her body near the University and her lodging house behind 13 Ashgrove under a pile of bricks. She was not a sex worker and that stoked up the fear in women again.

1980 In April Sutcliffe was arrested for Driving whilst under the influence of alcohol and then killed two more women whilst awaiting his trial. On 20th August he killed Marguerite Walls forty-seven and then on 17th November Jacqueline Hill a student at Leeds University whose body was found on an old bombsite near the Arndale Centre. He also attacked Uphadya Badara in Leeds on 24th September, Maureen Lea an art student was then attacked in the grounds of Leeds University on 25th October and sixteen year old Theresa Sykes in Huddersfield on Guy Fawkes night 5th November. On 25th November 1980 Sutcliffe's original partner in his first assault in 1969 reported him to the police as a suspect after various conversations they had had over the years but the information vanished in the pile of police paperwork already filling many boxes.

Sutcliffe was beaten several times whilst in prison with one beating resulting in the loss of sight in one eye. He died aged 74 on November 13th 2020 in the University Hospital of North Durham where he was serving his sentence. He had tested positive for COVID-19 but refused treatment.

Sutcliffe was married to Sonia Szurma in 1967, the marriage was childless and they bought and moved into 6 Garden Lane in Heaton, Bradford a house that she still owns.

****

1975 HAROLD SHIPMAN

Shipman was born on 14th January 1946 on a council estate in Nottingham. He was one of three children of Harold Shipman and Vera Shipman nee Brittan. A bright lad Shipman passed his eleven-plus and went onto High Pavement Grammar School in Nottingham where he became an accomplished athlete in long distance running and rugby and in his final year captained the school athletics team. The mental roots for his later serial killings of elderly people has been traced back to the death of his mother when he was seventeen. She suffered with lung cancer and in the terminal stages of her life had morphine administered by the family doctor to lessen the pain and passed away on 21st June 1963. At twenty years old Shipman married Primrose May Oxtoby and they went on to have 4 children. Shipman embarked on a medical career studying at Leeds School of Medicine and graduated in 1970 to work at Pontefract General Infirmary. In 1974 he took the position of General Practitioner at the Abraham Ormerod Medical Practice in Todmorden. Just one year into this position he was caught forging prescriptions for the drug pethidine for his own use, he was fined £600 and made to take a drug rehabilitation course in a York clinic. He went from the GP in Todmorden to another GP position at Donneybrook Medical Centre in Hyde, Manchester in1977. He stayed there throughout the 80s and in1993 established his own surgery at 21 Market Street becoming a highly respected member of the local community.

There were early indications that something was not right at Shipman's Surgery. In March 1998 Dr Linda Reynolds of the Donneybrook Surgery in Hyde told the South Manchester coroner, John Pollard that she had concerns at the high death rate of Shipman's patients and especially the large amount of cremation forms he was asking her to countersign as two GP signatures on each form was the law at the time. The police took a look but couldn't find any evidence of wrongdoing and closed their investigation in April 1998. The later Shipman Enquiry lay blame at the door of the Greater

Manchester Police for putting inexperienced officers on that investigation. Shipman carried on killing. In August the same year taxi driver John Shaw made his suspicions known when many of the elderly customers he took to the hospital who were in good health died in Shipman's care. Overall Shaw named 21 patients he suspected that Shipman murdered.

Kathleen Grundy was Shipman's last victim. She was found dead at home on June 24th 1998. Shipman was the last person to see her alive and also signed her death certificate citing old age as the cause. The daughter Angela Woodruff, who was a lawyer, set the alarm bells ringing when it transpired that a will had been made by her mother that the family solicitor had great concerns about. This will excluded Angela Woodruff and her children but left £386,000 to Shipman. At the solicitor's request Woodruff called in the police who exhumed Grundy's body and found traces of diamorphine (heroin) which was used to control pain in terminal cancer patients. Shipman claimed that Grundy had become an addict and showed police comments he had written about Grundy's addiction on his computerised medical records. Forensic examination of the computer showed they were actually written after her death. He was arrested on September 7th 1998 and a search of his house found a Brother typewriter that matched the print on the forged will. The police then set a major investigation in place and looked at fifteen specimen deaths that Shipman had certified. They discovered a regular pattern. Shipman would administer lethal doses of diamorphine, sign the patient's death certificate and then falsify their medical records to indicate they had been in poor health.

Shipman stood trial at Preston Crown Court in October 1999 charged with the murders of fifteen women between 1995 and 1998 by giving them lethal doses of diamorphine. The ladies were; Marie West, Irene Turner, Lizzie Adams, Jean Lilley, Ivy Thomas, Muriel Grimshaw, Marie Quinn, Kathleen Wagstaff, Bianka Pomfret, Norah Nuttall, Pamela Hillier, Maureen Ward, Winifred Mellor, Joan Melia and Kathleen Grundy. Grundy's was the only murder where Shipman stood to gain financially. The others lacked any motive. On January 31st 2000 the jury returned a verdict of guilty of murder on fifteen counts and one count of forgery. Mr Justice Forbes sentenced Shipman to life imprisonment on all fifteen counts with a recommendation he never be released plus a further four years for forging Grundy's will. Shipman was struck off by the General Medical Council and David Blunkett the Home Secretary confirmed the judge's recommendation of a whole life tariff.

Shipman always denied his guilt and never gave public statements or tried to appeal the sentences. His wife maintained his innocence even after the conviction. He hung himself in HM Prison Wakefield on 13th January 2004, the eve of his 58th birthday using bed sheets tied to the window bars. An autopsy was carried out and the body released to the family who kept it in a morgue for more than a year despite false reports of a funeral which the police had advised against knowing that any grave would be attacked. The family eventually had the body cremated on 19th March 2005 at Hutcliffe Wood Crematorium outside normal hours and only Primrose and the four children attended.

In January 2001 West Yorkshire Police investigated another twenty two West Yorkshire deaths and concluded that Shipman had killed two hundred and eighteen of his patients during his time at Todmorden and Hyde Surgeries. Many more deaths were of a similar nature but lacked enough evidence to be definitely Shipman's work. The majority of those attributed to him were elderly ladies with no health problems. A further report in 2005 found that four hundred and fifty nine people died whilst under Shipman's care between 1971 and 1998 but most could not be listed as murdered as Shipman was the only signature on the death certificate, the estimate of his probable victim count now rose to two hundred and fifty. At the time of his arrest Police seized over £10,000 of jewellery hidden in his garage and asked the families of his known victims to identify any they could. Primrose asked for the return of any unclaimed pieces and was given 66 pieces she claimed and a further 33 pieces that she said were not hers were sent to auction with Tameside Victim Support getting the money. Only one piece went to a victim's family who identified it with a photograph as proof of ownership. A memorial garden to Shipman's victims opened in Hyde Park, Hyde in 2005 named The Garden of Tranquillity. As a legal result of Shipman's case the organiser(s) of a funeral or a cremation have this question added on the form; 'Do you know or suspect that the death of the person who has died was violent or unnatural? Do you consider that there should be any further examination of the remains of the person who has died?'

****

1976 DONALD NEILSON

Donald Neilson 1936-2011 born Donald Nappey was nicknamed 'The Black Panther'. He was an armed robber, kidnapper and serial killer. Between 1971 and 1974 he murdered three men whilst robbing sub post offices and then in 1975 murdered Lesley Whittle an heiress who he kidnapped in Highley Shropshire.

Neilson got into burglary and robbing shops at the early age of twelve, two years after his mother died of cancer. He pursued a criminal lifestyle and married at eighteen whilst doing his National Service in the King's Own Yorkshire Light Infantry. His wife hated the army life and persuaded him to leave. They had a daughter, Kathryn in 1960 and four years later Neilson changed his name from Nappey to Neilson so she wouldn't have to endure the abuse he had suffered at school and in the army with the surname Nappey. This thoughtful action was totally opposite to the actions he was about to embark on. He was a clever burglar and committed over four hundred house burglaries without being caught in his early days of crime. He was clever and left a series of confusing clues for the police, for instance amongst his haul he would steal a radio and leave it in the open nearby and repeat that for a number of burglaries and then change to something else. The police would waste time trying to figure out why. After stealing guns and ammunition from a house in Cheshire he upped his game turning his attention to sub post offices where the take was considerably bigger than household items and was cash. He robbed 18 post offices between 1971 and 1974 and used violence when the owners tried to resist and fought back. He always wore a hood and spoke with a fake West Indian accent. The first three murders were in 1974 during sub post office robberies. He shot dead two sub-postmasters and the husband of a sub-postmistress as well as severely beating sub-postmistress Margaret Hayland who was able to give police a pretty accurate description of Neilson. He shot dead Donald Skepper in Harrogate, Derek Astin in Baxenden and Sidney Grayland (husband of Margaret) in Langley, West Midlands. All in 1974.

It was after the Baxenden murder that he got the nickname 'Black Panther' when Astin's wife Marion described him as 'so quick, he was like a panther' meaning his black clothing. The local papers ran with lurid headlines like 'Where is the Black Panther'.

Neilson was only linked to these murders after he was out checking a ransom trail he was to use in the later Lesley Whittle kidnap and was approached by security guard Gerald Smith because of his suspicious behaviour and shot Smith six times. Forensic examination of the bullets linked them and the gun that murdered both Astin and Grayland.

George Whittle was a multi millionaire owner of a coach and transport business in Highley, Shropshire. When he died his fortune was left to his mistress and their children, Ronald and Lesley. The legal family started a court case to secure the money disputing Whittle's will.

It is thought that Neilson read of this and planned to take some of this fortune by kidnapping and holding for ransom the daughter and that he planned it for some time. In January 1975 he took seventeen year old Lesley from her bedroom at night leaving a £500,000 ransom demand note. The family decided to pay but a series of police cock ups meant her brother Ronald was unable to deliver the money at the time and place Neilson had demanded and nothing more was heard.

Lesley Whittle's hanging body was found on 7th March at the bottom of a drainage shaft in Bathpool Park, Kidsgrove, Staffordshire. She had been left tethered around the neck on a ledge from which forensic speculation suggested she had fallen off or Neilson had pushed her off after he panicked thinking that police were closing in on him on the night the ransom was supposed to have been paid and wasn't. At the trial Neilson's Defence said that the conditions he kept Whittle in were not those of a cold blooded murderer. The noose around Whittle's neck was padded for comfort and the ledge she was on was cushioned with a mattress. The Defence noted that had the tether around her neck not snagged on a stanchion when she slipped off the ledge she would not have died as her feet were swinging just 6 inches above the bottom of the shaft. The drop from the ledge to the shaft floor was six feet eleven inches, the tether was nine foot long. Defence also said Neilson had provided Whittle with chicken soup, spaghetti and meatballs, fish and chips and polo mints as well as a sleeping bag, blankets and books, all were found in the shaft.

Neilson was arrested in December 1975 after a man carrying a holdall was spotted by two police officers in a Panda car walking on the A60 out of Mansfield. He hid his face as he passed them which raised their suspicions so they called him over and questioned him. Neilsen took a sawn off shot-gun from his bag and ordered one of the policemen into the back seat and took his place next to the driver with the shot-gun held against him. Neilsen ordered them to drive to Rainworth. The driver explained they were going the wrong way and would have to turn round at the next junction, Neilson agreed. The driver made the turn very sharply, violently swinging the car left and right, the gun dropped a few inches and the other constable pushed it up and away from the driver who stepped on the brake. The car came to a halt outside The Junction Chip Shop in Rainham as the gun went off. The driver fell out of the vehicle and ran towards the chippy shouting for help. Two men ran from the queue and helped the policemen overpower Neilsen and handcuff him. The locals realising it was the Black Panther set about beating him and he had to be protected from them before police help arrived.

In July 1976 Neilson was convicted of the kidnapping and murder of Lesley Whittle and given a life sentence. Three weeks later he was convicted of the murders of the two postmasters and the husband of a postmistress. All in all he got five life sentences plus a further sixty-one years for kidnapping Lesley Whittle and a further ten years for blackmailing her mother. Another three sentences of ten years each were given for the two burglaries from where he stole guns and ammunition and for possessing a firearm with intent to endanger life. All the sentences were to run concurrently. He was acquitted of the attempted murders of Margaret Grayland and PC White the panda car driver but found guilty of the lesser charges of grievous bodily harm on Margaret Grayland and possession of a shotgun with intent to endanger life of the second policeman. A further charge as mentioned above for the attempted murder of security guard Gerald Smith who he shot six times whilst checking his ransom escape route was dropped due to legal complications. Smith died just over a year later.

After the sentencing Defence Counsel Gray found Neilson huddled in a corner of the remand cell below the courthouse crying with remorse for Whittle.

Neilson's wife Irene became worried on the night he was caught when he didn't return home and fearing he had been arrested so she burnt over fifty stolen postal orders in the fire grate which forensics were able to reconstruct well enough to press charges. She claimed to have been forced by Neilson into cashing POs in post offices over a large area and that she was afraid of him. An excuse her solicitor and lawyers pressed forward trying to secure probation rather than a custodial sentence. It didn't work and she got twelve months. It was appealed but the appeal failed and she served eight months before being released and it is alleged made a fortune selling the story to the tabloid press.

Donald Neilson died on 18th December 2011 after suffering breathing difficulties at Norwich Prison and being transferred to Norfolk and Norwich University Hospital. The whereabouts of Irene are unknown.

****

1977 ARCHIBALD HALL

'The Killer Butler'

Hall was born in Glasgow on 17th June 1924 and died in prison 16th September 2002. At the time of his death he was the oldest person serving a whole life tariff in UK prisons.

Hall started on his criminal ways at the young age of just fifteen by stealing and house breaking. He was bisexual and left Glasgow to enter the gay scene in London using the money from his thieving to pay the fare but came unstuck when jewellery stolen in Scotland was recognised by a dealer in London and he was arrested. Inside prison he decided he wanted to mix in the aristocratic circles when released which would afford him better pickings from house breaking and so he studied antiques, etiquette and took elocution lessons to lose his broad Scottish accent. On being released Hall began using the name Roy Fontaine after the actress Joan Fontaine who he was a great admirer of and forged references stating that he was an honest and trustworthy butler. He gained employment as a butler but was returned to prison several times when caught stealing from his employers.

When released in1975 Hall travelled back to Scotland with his fake references and got employment as a butler with Margaret Hudson a Dowager and the widow of Sir Austin Hudson who had been an MP. She lived at Kirleton House, Dumfriesshire. His initial reason in taking the position was to steal any jewellery but he found he liked the lady and the job and refrained from any theft. He then got an old friend David Wright, from his prison days, a job as gamekeeper on the estate in 1977. They fell out when Wright stole some of the Dowager's jewellery and refused to put it back and threatened to tell her about Hall's own criminal past and his fake references if Hall reported him. This would be too much for Hall who was becoming the Lady Dowager's trusted confidant and could see a handsome payout coming his way when she died so he shot Wright and buried him beside a stream in the grounds. Lady Hudson did finally discover Hall's past and he was sacked from his job and travelled back to London where he took on his old criminal antics of theft and forgery getting a butler's position to eighty-two year old Walter Scott-Elliot who had been MP for Accrington and his sixty year old wife Dorothy. Hall's big plan was to rob the wealthy couple and retire on the proceeds. He enlisted another criminal Michael Kitto as an accomplice but their plan was discovered by Scott-Elliot's wife who was going to the police but Kitto suffocated her with a pillow before the pair drugged Scott-Elliot and with the help of the housekeeper Mary Coggle, who they promised a good payout when they sold the Scott-Elliot's antiques, they drove the drugged husband and dead wife up to Scotland where they buried Dorothy in Braco, Perthshire, and then strangled the unconscious Walter and buried him in woods at Tomich, Inverness. Mary Coggle had left London with a suitcase of Her Ladyship's clothes and took to wearing them which brought some unwanted attention on the trio. She refused to get rid of an expensive fur coat which Hall thought would be incriminating evidence if they came under suspicion for the deaths so together with Kitto he killed Mary Coggle with a poker and dumped her body in a stream at Middlebie, Dumfriesshire. On December 27th 1977 her body was found by a shepherd searching for lost sheep. Hall had a holiday home in Cumbria and they fled there only to find Hall's half-brother Donald already living there. He had been recently released from a sentence for sexually assaulting children and no love was lost between the brothers. Hall and Kitto devised a plan to get rid of Donald by telling him their next robbery was a big one where they would have to tie up a guard and persuaded Donald to let them practice tying knots on him. Once Donald was tied up Hall rendered him unconscious with chloroform before drowning him in the bath. They decided they would once again drive upto to Scotland to dump the body. This was a mistake. Hall was becoming very jittery about the murders so far and thought it was a bad sign that the number plate of their car had three '9's in it 999, the police emergency phone number so he had Kitto replace it with a false one which of course didn't match the number on the tax disc which was displayed in the windscreen in those days. They checked in at the Blenheim House Hotel in Berwick as the weather was atrocious and they didn't fancy driving out into the wilds to bury Donald's body in the driving snow. The hotel owner didn't like their attitude and evasive answers to his registration questions and fearing he would not be paid he called the local police who soon noticed the discrepancy between the tax disc and number plate. Hall and Kitto were taken in for questioning and a search of the car revealed Donald's body in the boot. Kitto was arrested but Hall made a bid for freedom through a lavatory window but was caught at a roadblock in Haddington.

Police enquiries connected the car and the pair to a report from an antique dealer in Newcastle-under-Lyme who had reported the pair for offering him antique silver at well under the market value. The car was traced to Walter Scott-Elliot's address in London and when the police forced entry they found it ransacked and with blood spatters on floors and walls. The link between this murder and Mary Coggle's was soon apparent as her body had already been found and she had been previously registered as Scott-Elliot's housekeeper. It was established on previous evidence collated when Coggle's body was found that two men and lady had stayed at a hotel a few nights before her body had been discovered but on the second night only the two men booked in.

Hall tried to commit suicide whist in police custody but in the end after continual questioning he admitted the murders and took police to the three burial sites where the bodies were exhumed. Hall and Kitto were charged with five murders.

Hall was convicted of four murders with that of Dorothy Scott-Elliot ordered to lie on the file. His sentence was life imprisonment with a recommendation he never be released. Kitto was sentenced to life for three murders and was in some way quite lucky as Hall confessed to police that he was planning to kill Kitto as well. Hall published an autobiography *A Perfect Gentleman* in 1999 and died of a stroke in Kingston Prison Portsmouth in 2002.

1978 DENNIS NILSEN

Not to be confused with Donald Nielsen, Dennis Andrew Nilsen murdered at least fifteen male victims between 1978 and 1983. Many of the corpses he kept to perform necrophiliac acts on. He was only caught when the human body parts he disposed of blocked the drains where he lived and the drain cleaning company alerted the police.

Nilsen was from Strichen, Aberdeenshire. His parents divorced because of his father's alcoholism when he was four. He lived for a short time with his grandparents until his mother remarried and took him back. He later insisted that his serial killing life style was caused by viewing his grandfather's body at the morgue after he died and the many lectures on sins of the flesh his step father and mother gave him as a child.

He joined the Army in 1961 and became a cook serving abroad in Cyprus, Aden and Germany. After leaving the Army he joined the Police in 1972 for a brief time and then moved to London and went into the civil service working at jobcentres. During this time he had many short relationships with men and suffered feelings of loneliness which these relationships did not cure. He was looking for a long relationship and this need bizarrely translated into why later on he would keep a corpse for a period of time.

In 1974 Nilsen's life was one of cruising gay bars where he met a man called David Gallichan who came home with Nilsen and stayed. After a while they moved into the infamous 195 Melrose Avenue. They were very happy for two years with Nilsen calling Gallichan 'twinkle' but Gallichan grew bored with Nilsen and both started bringing home other men as the relationship fell apart and eventually Gallichan left. Nilsen sank into a daily round of gay bars or staying home with a bottle of rum for comfort. This led to victim number one (see victims list later) Stephen Dean Holmes, who he met in the Cricklewood Arms pub and took home, both drinking themselves into a stupor. When Nilsen woke the next morning he felt he couldn't let Holmes leave his life and wanted him as a companion forever. He murdered him and put Holmes body under the floorboards where it remained for eight months.

His victims were all men who led insular lives, mostly students or the homeless that he picked up in bars and brought to his house for sex or just for company. After strangling or drowning them in a bath he used his butcher skills learned in the army to dismember their bodies. Many of the body parts were burnt on bonfires in his back garden.

His downfall came after he moved into an upstairs flat in 23 Cranley Gardens, Muswell Hill, London. He continued his murdering but with no back garden he had to find alternative ways to dispose of his victims' bodies. He had a suitcase of human body organs in his wardrobe and many plastic bags of body parts hidden under the floorboards. The neighbours complained of the smell so he turned to flushing the remains down the toilet which eventually blocked the sewage outlet of the house. The company called in to clear the blockage, Dyno-rod, became suspicious of the flesh like substance causing it and told Nilsen a supervisor would take a look the next day. The next day they found it had been cleared overnight which raised bigger suspicions and they called the police. Examples of bone fragments and skin taken from the drain were forensically diagnosed as human and in 1983 Nilsen was arrested on suspicion of multiple murders. Nilsen was unable to put a figure on the number of people he had killed but said it was 'quite a few'. The search of his flat found three heads in a sink cupboard and thirteen more bodies in his old house at 195 Melrose Avenue, Cricklewood.

It was noted by the press at his trial that he seemed 'far away' and totally unaffected by the prosecution's descriptions of his crimes. At the Old Bailey his defence pleaded diminished responsibility to try and get a charge of manslaughter but Nilsen was found guilty of six murders and two attempted murders. He was sentenced to life imprisonment on which the Home Secretary added a 'whole life' tariff.

NILSEN'S VICTIM LIST.

Victim number one was fourteen year old Stephen Dean Holmes killed on December 30th 1978. Nilsen picked him up at a gay bar took him home, strangled him with a tie until he was unconscious and then drowned him by submerging his head in a bucket of water.

Number two; Canadian student Kenneth Ockendon was strangled during a sex act with Nilsen. He was listed on the Missing Persons police data list.

Number three; Martyn Duffey a 16 year old homeless boy from Liverpool who accepted an invitation in 1980 to lodge at Nilsen's place. Strangled into unconsciousness and drowned in the kitchen sink.

Number four; A male prostitute from Scotland named Billy Sutherland. Strangled by Nilsen's bare hands.

Number five; A male prostitute, but not able to be identified. Thought to be Asian.

Number six; All Nilsen could remember was that he was a young Irish labourer he met in a bar.

Number seven; Nilsen described him as a hippy type rough sleeper.

Number eight; Nilsen couldn't remember anything about him.

Number nine; Young Scottish man picked up in Soho pub.

Number ten; As number nine.

Number eleven; A young skinhead picked up in Piccadilly Circus with a 'cut here' tattoo around his neck. Nilsen hung his naked body in his bedroom for a day before putting him wrapped in plastic under the floorboards.

Number twelve; Malcolm Barlow found in poor condition in a doorway near Nilsen's home. Nilsen acted the Good Samaritan and called an ambulance. When Barlow was released from hospital the next day he went to thank Nilsen who invited him in and murdered him.

After number twelve in October 1981 Nilsen moved to Muswell hill. He could have been caught twice. A student he met in a Soho bar and took back awoke with a sore neck the next day and went to his doctor who diagnosed it as a strangulation attempt and advised he report Nilsen to the police. However afraid his sexual orientation would be disclosed the student decided not to.

Following this Nilsen brought home a drag queen from a pub in Camden who passed out being strangled and awoke whilst Nilsen was trying to drown him in the bath and managed to fight his way out. He didn't report it.

John Howlett the first victim in the Muswell Hill home. He apparently put up a fight and both had injuries before Howlett was eventually drowned and became the first body to be dismembered with parts being hidden around the flat and flushed down the toilet.

Graham Allen a homeless man met in Shaftesbury Avenue. Nilsen left Allen's body in the bath for 3 days before dismembering it and hiding bits around the flat and flushing parts down the toilet.

The final victim was drug addict Stephen Sinclair who Nilsen bought a hamburger after befriending him in Oxford Street. Taking Sinclair home Nilsen plied him with alcohol and heroin then strangled and dismembered the body. It was Sinclair's remains that blocked the drain outside Nilsen's property and first alerted the police to the crimes.

Nilsen is currently held at HMP Full Sutton maximum security prison in Yorkshire.

****

1979 GLYN DIX

This is a strange story. Dix was a hospital porter and on 2nd October 1979 he murdered his landlady, Pia Overbury, thirty-two, a married mother of two by tying her to a tree in woods near her Gloucestershire home, raping her and then shooting her in the head. On 20th October a lady walking her dog together with her children in woods at Hartpury in the Forest of Dean came upon the body hidden in undergrowth and police identified it as Pia Overbury. Cartridges and a gun were found at the scene. The gun was traced back to Dix who was questioned for some time, charged with murder and remanded in custody where he attempted to commit suicide. He was tried at Bristol Crown Court and sentenced to life in 1980. Whilst in prison he befriended cellmate Adam Langford who was serving a sentence for multiple motoring offences. Langford had visits from his mother Hazel who felt sorry for Dix who had no visitors and the two became regular pen pals. On 5th November 1999 Dix married Hazel Langford whilst on day release. After his release in 2001 on parole they set up home together with Hazel's children who they managed to convince that Dix was not guilty of Overbury's murder and had been framed by Overbury's husband. On Saturday 19th June 2004 Hazel Dix's son Adam came home to the house at Abbeydale, Redditch, Worcestershire, at 4pm and found Glyn Dix kneeling naked over his mother's dismembered body with a knife in his hand. Dix told Adam, 'we had a little argument'. Dix and Hazel had had sex and then argued about which TV channel to watch. Dix had stabbed her multiple times and then used a knife, hacksaw and scissors to cut Hazel's body in to sixteen pieces. He had sawn off arms and legs, and cut out the heart, liver and kidneys using garden tools and kitchen knives.

Dix was sentenced to life in a high security hospital at Merseyside. In 2008 the Home secretary added a 'whole life no parole' tariff to the sentence. Dix died at Ashworth Secure Hospital on 1st January 2014 aged 86.

****

1979 MARK ROBINSON

Currently serving a whole life tariff in Wakefield Prison, Mark Robinson is known as one of the county's most dangerous inmates.

He was seventeen when he strangled Patricia Wagner and left her body to be found in the living room of her council house in Newbury Way, Billingham by her eight year old daughter. A team of 50 detectives started a manhunt for the killer. The house showed no visible signs of a forced entry and the back door and window were unlocked. Wagner had got home at 11.30pm the previous evening after spending time with her mother, who lived close by, and then making a transatlantic phone call to her husband Glenn who worked on American oil rigs.

Known for being a chirpy lady who liked to go out to bars and night clubs in the Stockton and Hartlepool area the police concentrated their efforts on interviewing the clubbers of the area. A few doors down one of Mrs Wagner's neighbours Mark Robinson had come home on leave from the RAF for the Spring Bank Holiday and had been seen walking towards Wagner's home less than two hours before she was last seen alive.

Under caution Robinson told police he had indeed gone to Wagner's house as he wanted sex and knew she was, as he put it, 'a good thing.' He had pretended to her that he had mistaken her house for his and they talked before Wagner invited him in and agreed to have sex. However Robinson had gone off the idea after she had told him about her prostitute past and said he told her he was going to leave but Wagner insisted he stay with her or she would tell his mother that he had visited for sex. Robinson claimed he called her 'a slut' and tried to leave but Wagner hit him and grabbed his head. To protect himself he punched her to the floor and lost his temper pulling a lamp flex round her neck had strangled her. This tied in with a post-mortem that revealed Wagner died from asphyxia and had facial injuries including a broken nose. It had been a ferocious attack.

Robinson was sentenced to a ten year prison term. When he was released in 1989 he met Sharon Morely in Wakefield and started a relationship. The couple moved to Billingham and arguments started as Sharon was unhappy there and wanted to move back to Wakefield and her social circle. On September 19th 1989 Robinson stabbed twenty-five year old Sharon to death after finding a photo of her former boyfriend in her belongings. This was just seven months after being released from his previous murder charge. Newcastle Crown Court sentenced him to life behind bars with a whole life tariff in place. In 2005 his violent temper caused him more trouble at Long Lartin jail in Worcestershire where he punched an officer whilst being led from a prison van to the cells on his first day, and then whilst working as a kitchen cleaner in the jail, he had argued with an officer when told to empty a rubbish bin. When the officer opened the door for Robinson take out the bin Robinson punched him unconscious and fractured his cheekbone. A further eight years was added to his life sentence for that attack. A few years later he attacked five prison officers in Wakefield prison after he accused them of cutting down his bread ration. All five needed A&E treatment. He was now upgraded to 'dangerous' and kept in his cell twenty-three hours a day. A further three years was added to his sentence.

****

1981 ROBERT BLACK

Born in Grangemouth, Scotland on 21st April 1947 Robert Black was the illegitimate son of Jessie Black and an unknown father. His mother emigrated and Black was fostered to an experienced middle aged couple called Tulip in Lochleven at six months old. He took their surname and began to exhibit a violent and aggressive nature at an early age. He vandalised his school and because of his name 'Tulip' was bullied by elder children and in turn he bullied those younger than himself. At five years old he played doctors and nurses with girls his own age and compared their genitalia which Black later said gave him the idea that he should have been born a girl. He had a compulsive interest in female genitalia and took to inserting objects into his own anus, a fetish he carried into his adult life. The Tulips both died by 1958 and he was moved to another foster family in the area and committed his first known sexual assault on a young girl in a public lavatory. His foster mother reported the offence to the Social Services and had him taken from her home. Black was put into a mixed-sex children's home in Falkirk where he began to expose himself to girls and one time forcibly removed a girl's underwear. He was removed and sent to Red House care Home, a strict, all male home in Musselburgh. Here he was sexually abused by a staff member who forced him to perform fellatio. The staff member was dismissed and Black moved on again, this time to a boy's home in Greenock where he reached age 16 and was able to get a job as a butcher's delivery boy, later claiming to have fondled up to 40 young girls if they were alone in the house when he called with a delivery. However, this may be wishful thinking as no assaults were ever reported.

One summer day in 1963 Black took a seven year old girl who was playing in a park into a deserted building on the pretext of showing her some kittens where he held her by the throat until she lost consciousness and then masturbated over her. He was arrested the following day and charged with lewd and libidinous behaviour. The psychiatrist that examined him said it was a 'one-off' and he was not in need of any treatment. Black received a verbal warning about his behaviour and the charge left on file. Black moved to Grangemouth and took lodgings with an elderly couple and work at a builder's supply company. He formed a good relationship with a local girl who refused to marry him because of his unusual sexual demands and she ended their relationship. In 1966 his landlords found out that he had sexually molested their nine year old granddaughter whenever she had visited the property whilst he was there. They evicted him but to save the girl any further trauma they didn't press charges or even inform the police but told his employers. Black lost his job after that and moved back to Kinlochleven lodging with a married couple and their six year old daughter. With hindsight it's pretty obvious what would happen, and it did. Within a year his landlords informed the police that Black had repeatedly molested their daughter. He pleaded guilty to three counts of indecent assault against a child and was sentenced to a year at Polmont Borstal in Brighton, a specialist home for serious young offenders.

In September 1968 six months after being released from Polmont Black moved to London, took lodgings in a bedsit near Kings Cross and took several casual jobs never settling down to any type of career path. One of the jobs was lifeguard at Hornsey swimming pool which only lasted a few weeks before he was fired for fondling a young girl, again no charges were brought. He frequented dodgy bookshops and in one at Kings Cross made friends with a contact who provided him with child pornography in book and magazine form from which he later progressed to videos of graphic child sexual abuse. He also took to taking discreet photos of young girls, mainly at swimming pools which he developed himself and kept in suitcases together with his growing collection of child pornography.

He moved to Stamford Hill, lodging with a Scottish couple Edward and Kathy Rayson where he remained until his arrest in July 1990.

Black enjoyed driving and bought a white Fiat van in the mid 70s to enable him to get more delivery work. In 1976 he got a permanent job as a van driver with Poster, Dispatch and Storage in Hoxton who delivered cinema posters nationwide. To the firm he was an asset as many of their married drivers refused the long distance overnight work but not Black. This job enabled Black to get a good knowledge of the UK road network and later be able to kidnap a child in one part of the country and dispose of their body hundreds of miles away in another part, it was ideal for him. He also took to wearing disguises and growing a beard or moustache which could be shaved off and also of completely shaving his head. He had several significant spectacle frames and covered the rear windows of his van.

Nine year old Jennifer Cardy was Black's first murder victim. She was abducted on 12th August 1981 as she cycled to a friend's house in Ballinderry, N Ireland. She never arrived and the alarm was raised by her mother. Cardy's bicycle was found a mile from her home hidden amongst leaves and bracken. Its stand was down signifying she had stopped to talk to her abductor. A massive search involving 200+ police and volunteers found nothing more. Her body was found by two anglers in a reservoir in Hillsborough six days later. The reservoir was near to a lay-by, just 16 miles from Cardy's home on a main Belfast to Dublin road. A road frequented by long distance lorry and delivery drivers. The pathologist noted signs of sexual abuse on her body and the autopsy found she had been strangled and drowned. Her watch had stopped at 5.40pm. Black's second murder victim was eleven year old Susan Maxwell who lived on the English-Scottish border at Cornhill-on-Tweed. She was taken on 30th July 1982 as she walked home after playing tennis in Coldstream. She was last seen alive crossing the Tweed bridge. Three hundred officers plus numerous dogs were assigned to the search for Maxwell over 80 square miles of rough countryside and every house within it. The only clue was that several people remembered a white van in the area. On 12th August her body was found covered with undergrowth and clothed except for her underwear and shoes. She had been bound and gagged but the precise time of death could not be determined because of the decomposition of the body.

Her underwear was neatly folded under her head suggesting a sexual assault but that was not able to be determined. The inquest concluded that Maxwell had been killed shortly after being snatched and as Black's delivery schedule for that time (later examined by police) took in Edinburgh, Dundee and Glasgow with the final delivery close to midnight on 30th July she would have been alive or dead in his van until the following day when he returned to London hiding the body beside the A518 near Uttoxeter where it had been found. This was 264 miles from where Maxwell was abducted. Caroline Hogg was Black's third and youngest victim. She disappeared from outside her Beach Lane Home in the Edinburgh suburb in the evening of 8th July 1983. The search was the biggest ever mounted by the Scottish police at that time with some 2000 members of the public plus 50 members of the Scots Fusiliers and the police taking part. It made UK headline news and police brought in nine known paedophiles who were in the area at the time for questioning, all were eliminated. Witnesses came forward who had seen an unkempt man wearing horn rimmed glasses watching Caroline and then following her to a fairground. Fourteen year old Jennifer Bond had seen the couple sitting on a bench and heard Hogg say 'yes please' to the man before they walked to the fairground holding hands. The man paid 15pence for Hogg to ride a carousel as he watched. Hogg must have been in the back of Black's van for at least 24 hours as he delivered posters to Glasgow after the abduction and bought fuel in Carlisle early the following day. On the 18th July Hogg's naked body was found in a ditch close to the M1 motorway in Twycross, three hundred and ten miles from her home and just twenty four miles from where Maxwell's body had been found a year before. Decomposition and insect activity on the body made the cause and time of death difficult to determine with the nearest estimation being that it had been where it was found on or after July 12th. Black had made a delivery to Bedworth on that date. The absence of clothing suggested a sexual motive.

Staffordshire and Leicestershire detectives met and decided that Hogg's and Maxwell's murderer were committed by the same person because of the similar distance between abduction and where the bodies were found. Cardy's murder was not linked with them until 2009. The investigation concentrated on long distance lorry drivers, delivery drivers or sales representatives who would cover such distances in their everyday jobs. Numerous companies with transport links between Scotland and the Midlands, both ways, were looked at and their drivers questioned yielding no firm results. The Chief Constables of the four forces now involved appointed the assistant chief constable of Northumbria, Hector Clark to liaise the operations and take overall charge. Because of the clogging up of the index card system in the Yorkshire Ripper case and over 500,000 index cards already filed in the Maxwell case Clark brought in the new computer information technology system known as HOLMES where all information was entered onto a data base and which all nationwide police forces could access and cross check. This system expanded to hold information on 189,000 people, 220,000 vehicles and details of over 60,000 interviews.

On 26th March 1986 ten year old Sarah Harper went missing from Morley in Leeds having left her home to go to the corner shop for a loaf of bread. The shop owner confirmed she had bought the bread and that a balding man had followed her into and out of the shop. Her family held a quick search of the area when she failed to return home and then alerted the police. A full search was initiated with 100 officers doing a house to house search across Morley in 3000 properties, 10,000 leaflets were printed and distributed, 1400 witness statements taken and the surrounding area searched by police and 200 local citizens. Police frogmen searched nearby Tingley reservoir. It was established by eyewitness accounts that a white transit van had been in the area at the time Sarah had gone missing. West Yorkshire police sent a telex to all other forces with the details. On 19th April Sarah's partially clothed body, gagged and bound was found floating in the River Trent near Nottingham, 70 miles from her home. The autopsy showed she had died between 5 and 8 hours after last being seen alive and the cause of death was drowning. Injuries to her face and neck had more than likely rendered her unconscious prior to being thrown into the water. She had been the victim of a sustained and violent sexual assault. A few days later a witness told West Yorkshire police he had seen a white van with a stocky, balding man standing by the passenger door on 26th March in the evening parked beside the River Soar at Ratcliffe on Soar. The Soar is a tributary to the Trent and this witness was taken very seriously. Later company records show Black had refuelled at Newport Pagnell the following afternoon and it is thought likely he had driven to Ratcliffe on Soar, thrown Harper's body into the water in the late evening on the day of the abduction or early the following day. The murders of Maxwell, Hogg and Harper were now showing similarities, all had been young white females, taken from the north of England and found dead in the midlands with little effort being made to hide their bodies.

Following the murder of Sarah Harper six police forces were now involved and Hector Clark moved his HQ to Wakefield. On 21 April 1986 the Head of Scotland Yard's Criminal Intelligence Branch Phillip Corbett held a meeting to discuss how best to share information between the forces and to re-open nineteen other unsolved cases of murdered children. He also contacted the FBI to ask for a psychological profile of the murderer. Psychological Profiling was in its infancy in the USA but getting results. It was not part of the UK police tool-box at the time.

The US profiling described the killer as a white male aged between thirty and forty who was a classic loner. Unkempt in appearance and the recipient of less than twelve years formal education, he probably lived alone in rented accommodation in a deprived neighbourhood. His killings were motivated by a sexual urge and he would have a fixation with child pornography and more than likely engaged in necrophilia with his victim's bodies before disposing of them.

On 23rd April 1988 Black attempted to abduct fifteen year old Teresa Thornhill in the district of Radford in Nottingham. Thornhill had been out in the local park with her boyfriend Andrew Beeston and other teenagers before they walked home. They parted at the end of Norton Street where she noticed a blue Transit van which had stopped ahead of her. Black had sold his white transit and bought a blue one in 1988. The driver got out, raised the bonnet and asked Thornhill, 'Can you fix engines?' Thornhill said she could not and began to walk faster. Black clasped his arms around her, covered her mouth and attempted to drag her into his vehicle. Thornhill fought back kicking him and squeezed his testicles which caused him to loosen his grip enough that she could bite his arm and start shouting. Her boyfriend, Andrew Beeston, heard her and ran towards the van shouting ' Let go of her you fat bastard'. Black let Thornhill go and she fell onto the road. Black then jumped back into the driver's seat and drove off. Thornhill and Beeston ran to Thornhill's home and told her parents what had happened and they immediately phoned the police. It is thought that because Teresa Thornhill was short for her fifteen years Black may have thought she was younger, he hadn't reckoned with a strong young fifteen year old that would fight back.

On the 14th July 1990 Black's abduction career came to an end. David Herkes, a 53 year old retired postmaster was mowing his front lawn in Stow when he saw a blue Transit van slow to a stop on the opposite side of the road. The driver got out and started to clean the windscreen as the six year old daughter of Herkes neighbour walked by. As Herkes stooped to clear the grass from his mower blades he saw under the van and on the far side the girls feet lifted from the pavement. Herkes stood back up and saw the driver pushing something into the van passenger seat and then clambering over it to the driver's seat, closing the passenger door and driving off. Herkes realised what had happened, ran to the girl's home and her mother rang the police. Within minutes six police cars were with Herkes who had taken the van's registration number and as they talked the van came back towards them along the same road. An officer stepped out and it halted. They dragged Black from the driver's seat and handcuffed him face down on the road. They released the victim from where Black had tied her up and then tied her inside a sleeping bag in the back of the van. A doctor later found she had been the subject of a serious sexual assault. Black's intention had been to make a final scheduled delivery to Galashiels before further abusing the girl and almost certainly killing her. Black admitted a sexual assault on the girl when interviewed at Selkirk police station and was remanded in custody and charged with child abduction. His van was found to contain various ropes, restraining devices, hoods and tape plus a Polaroid camera, girls clothing, a mattress and sexual aids. His Stamford Hill lodgings were also searched and a large collection of child pornography in all types of media was found plus sex aids and girls clothing. On August 10th 1990 Black was tried at the Edinburgh High Court charged with abduction and sexual assault of the Stow schoolgirl. Black pleaded guilty and was sentenced to life imprisonment. The jury were told that had Black not been stopped by the police the girl in the sleeping bag would have suffocated within half an hour.

A fortnight after the Stow trial Hector Clark conducted a six hour interview with Black who he was sure was responsible for the murder of the other young girls. Black was forthcoming about his sexual experiences, self abuse and his attraction towards young girls and boasted that he had sexually assaulted at least 30 girls between the 1960s and 80s. He clammed up when asked about other murders and unsolved cases of abduction and murder. The interviewers told Black that they had solid evidence that he was in Portobello during the time of Caroline Hogg's abduction and witnesses had identified him from photos of him taken during the early 80s in his possessions. He then shut up or evaded direct answers to all their questions. He then refused to co-operate with any further questioning.

The travel records of Black's deliveries held by Poster, Dispatch and Storage plus petrol receipts he had given them to claim the money back were closely examined and put Black close to all the abduction and retrieved body areas near to the time or on the day they occurred. A delivery in Morley, Yorkshire was just 100yds from Sarah Harper's home. It was discovered that on many occasions when returning to London Black had slept overnight at his landlord's son's house in Donisthorpe very close to where all three bodies had been discovered. A further laborious investigation of several million petrol slips archived on microfilm by the credit card companies Poster, Dispatch and Storage had accounts with showed Black's signature on some with each instance being near to and shortly before or after each girl had been snatched. In March 1992 Hector Clark took his evidence to the CPS who decided there was enough to go ahead and prosecute Black. In pre-trial hearings Black's defence lawyers argued against all the charges being put as one and of the prosecution being allowed to show any similarity between the murders and Black's modus operandi. The Judge ruled against these motions.

On 13th April 1994 Black appeared at Moot Hall, Newcastle upon Tyne charged with ten charges of kidnap, murder, attempted kidnap and unlawful burial of a body. He pleaded not guilty to all the charges. The judge gave his final instructions to the jury on 16th May. They deliberated for two days before returning verdicts of guilty on three counts of kidnapping, three counts of murder, three counts of preventing the lawful burial of a body and one count of attempted abduction. (this referred to Teresa Thornhill). He was sentenced to life imprisonment on each charge with a 35 year recommendation on each to be served concurrently. He was taken to Wakefield Prison segregation unit as a Category A prisoner.

The courts were not finished with Black who was summoned to Armagh Crown Court on 22nd September 2001 charged with the murder of Jennifer Cardy. He pleaded not guilty. The evidence produced was once again petrol receipts and delivery times. The trial lasted six weeks with the jury returning a guilty verdict for Cardy's abduction, sexual assault and murder. Black received a further life sentence with a minimum 25 years. The eight-year, nationwide inquiry which culminated in the 1990 arrest of Robert Black proved to be one of the longest, most exhaustive and costly British murder investigations of the 20th century. By the time investigators had amassed enough evidence to convince the Crown Prosecution Service to charge Black with the three child murders and the attempted abduction of Thornhill, the dossier they had assembled was estimated to weigh 22 tons. The total cost of the inquiry is estimated to be £12 million.

An appeal against the sentences, all of them, was launched by Black in 1994 and thrown out on the first day by the Judge. It was alleged that many an appeal that stood no chance was launched purely for the lawyers to gain income from the legal aid budget. Black never admitted any of the abductions or murders although he had no chance of freedom. He was attacked a couple of times in prison and suffered superficial injuries and died from a heart attack on 12th January 2016 aged 68 at HMP Maghaberry. He was cremated at Roselawn Crematorium, Belfast on

29th January with nobody other than prison officials present and his ashes scattered at sea that February. Police are convinced that Black committed more murders before being convicted with estimates of eight plus being the best educated guess.

Black has now been linked to 14 further child murders and abductions in the UK, Ireland and Europe between 1969 and 1989. His murders were not limited to the UK.

On 8th April 1969 April Fabb age thirteen was abducted whilst cycling from Metton, Norfolk to her sister's home in Roughton. Her bike was found in a field on the route but no body has ever been found.

On 21st May 1973 Christine Markham age nine was last seen walking to school at Scunthorpe. No body has been found. Black was questioned about her in 2004.

On 19th August 1978 Genette Tate age thirteen was abducted whilst on her newspaper delivery round in Aylesbeare, Devon. He bicycle was discovered in a country lane by two girls who had been talking to her a few minutes before but her body has never been found. Black was delivering multiple drops in Devon and Cornwall at the time. Devon and Cornwall police had prepared a case to go to court accusing Black of Tate's abduction and murder when he died in prison.

On 28th July 1979 Suzanne Lawrence age fourteen left her sister's home in Harold Hill, London and was never seen again. No body has been found and Lawrence was added to Black's possible victim list as well as being added to serial killer Peter Tobin's probable list.

On 16th June 1980 Patricia Morris age fourteen disappeared from the grounds of her school in Hounslow. Her body was found in Hounslow Heath two days later, she was fully clothed and had been strangled with no sexual assault. Levi Bellfield has claimed responsibility for the murder but he would have been 12 at the time so a great deal of doubt exists as to his claim.

On 4th November 1981 Pamela Hastie age 16 was found strangled and bludgeoned in Johnstone, Renfrewshire. A single witness saw a man matching

Black's description at the time near the scene but police do not think it was him as he was not near the area at the time and she was older than his normal victims.

IRELAND

On 18th March 1977 Mary Boyle age six disappeared whilst visiting her grandparents in Ballyshannon. Black was in County Donegal at the time having been charged with after-hours drinking in Annagry a village in the Rosses District of Donegal. No body has been found.

EUROPE

On 20th June 1985 Silke Garben age ten disappeared on her way to the dentist in Detmold. Her body was found in a stream close to a British Army Base. She had been violently sexually assaulted and strangled although the cause of death was drowning. Black is known to have delivered posters to this British Army Base on the day of Garben's disappearance.

On 11th May 1989 Ramona Herling age eleven disappeared walking to a swimming baths in Bad Driburg. No body has been found.

HOLLAND

On 5th August 1986 Cheryl Morren age seven disappeared walking to a friend's house in Ijmuiden. Her body has never been found. Black made many personal trips to nearby Amsterdam to buy child pornography. He is a strong suspect in this case.

FRANCE

On 5th May 1987 Virginie Delmas age ten disappeared from Neuilly-sur-Marne. Her naked body was found in Mareuil-les-Meaux in an orchard on 9th October with her clothes folded beside her, an attribute Black often used. She had been strangled but decomposition of the body prevented any further pathology. Black was in and around the area at the time of her disappearance.

On 30th May 1987 Hemma Greedharry age ten disappeared on the way to a pottery class in Malakoff. Her body was found just two hours later in a car park in Chatillon. She had been raped, strangled and the body set alight. Black often used the road running alongside the car park when delivering to northern France.

On 3rd June 1987 Perrine Vigneron age seven went missing on her way to a card shop in Bouleurs. Her strangled body was found in a field in Chelles two days later with her clothes neatly folded beside her. A white van had been seen near the spot.

On 27th June 1987 Sabine Dumont age nine a Paris schoolgirl was last seen walking home from a book shop in Bievres. Her strangled and sexually assaulted body was found the next day in Vauhallan, North France. Black was named as primary suspect in 2011.

****

1983 ARTHUR HUTCHINSON

Hutchinson was already known to police when he murdered three people and raped one in Dore, Sheffield in 1983. He is serving a life sentence on a Home Office order that he never be released.

Before the murders Hutchinson had been in prison for a five year sentence for the attempted murder of his half brother. On 28th September 1983 he was arrested for burglary, theft and rape and taken to Selby Police Station where he jumped out of a toilet window and went on the run. Four weeks later on 23rd October he broke into the home of Basil Laitner 59, his wife Avril 55 and their son Richard 28, through an unlocked back garden patio window. After stabbing them all to death he raped their eighteen year old daughter Nicola and ran off. It had been the day of the Laitner's other daughter Suzanne's wedding and the reception had taken place in that very house.

Hutchinson left a palm print which was used to convict him after Nicola had identified him from his existing mug shot and forensic scientists matched a bite mark on a piece of cheese in the fridge to his teeth. He evaded capture for a fortnight living rough and was finally cornered on a farm in Hartlepool on 5th November 1983. At his trial he tried to blame a Sunday Mirror reporter Mike Barron of being the real killer. This trial was the first time a police video of the murder scene including the bodies was allowed to be shown to the jury. He was found guilty and sentenced to life imprisonment, minimum term eighteen years but the Home Secretary, Leon Brittan put him on a 'life means life' list.

In 2008 he appealed against the Home Secretary's ruling arguing that a whole life tariff breached his human rights. His appeal to the High Court was rejected. His lawyers lodged an appeal but it too was rejected. In 2015 he appealed to the Grand Chamber of the European Court who turned it down ruling that the Home Secretary was within his constitutional rights to impose a whole-life tariff in appropriate circumstances

DCI Mick Burdis who led the police in the case said that not once had Hutchinson shown any remorse. Hutchinson's own mother vowed never to see him again.

****

1985 JEREMY BAMBER

Convicted in 1985 of the now, infamous, 'White House Farm Murders' with his guilt or innocence being the subject of great debate ever since, including TV documentaries and books.

Bamber was born Jeremy Paul Marsham in Kensington, London in 1961 to Juliet Dorothy Wheeler, a clergyman's daughter, as the product of her affair with Army Sergeant Leslie Brian Marsham who worked at Buckingham Palace. Wheeler gave the baby up for adoption in its first year through the Church of England Children's Society. Nevill and June Bamber wealthy farmers at White House Farm, Tolleshunt D'Arcy in Essex adopted Bamber at 6 months old. This was their second adopted child having adopted a girl Sheila four years before. White House Farm was a large Georgian house that reflected the social standing and wealth of the Bambers. Nevill was a local Magistrate.

Bamber went to a private prep school, Maldon Court and then in 1970 was sent away as a boarder to Gresham's School in Norfolk. He left with no qualifications which caused heated rows within the family and was sent to Colchester 6th form college where he passed seven O Levels. His close friend at the time, Brett Collins, later claimed Bamber had told him he was repeatedly sexually assaulted aged eleven at Greshams and continued to have sexual relations with both men and women being popular with both. The family sent Bamber to Australia when he left school where he gave scuba diving lessons, and then to New Zealand where he was 'ripped off' by a heroin dealer and entered that world. He boasted to Brett Collins that he smuggled heroin and robbed a jewellery store in New Zealand and had to leave in a hurry after being sought for involvement in an armed robbery. Back in the UK he stayed away from the family and worked in the hospitality business and cafes for a while before agreeing to return to White House Farm and work on the farm. He resented the low wages but was given a car and a rent free cottage his father owned at 9 Head Street, Goldhanger three miles from the farm. He was also given eight percent of the family owned caravan site in Maldon.

Sometime before the murders he broke into and robbed the caravan park which was only later revealed at his murder trial when a girlfriend Julie Mugford gave evidence against him.

On the day of the murders, 7th August 1985, Bamber phoned the police at 3.30am telling them that his father had phoned him to say that Bamber's sister Sheila had got hold of his father's rifle and was going 'berserk' with it and to get the police. When the police forced entry into White House Farmhouse they found Sheila dead on her parent's bedroom floor with the rifle against her throat looking like suicide. June Bamber was found dead in the same room, Sheila's six year old twin sons were dead in their beds in another bedroom and Nevill Bamber shot dead in the kitchen downstairs. Twenty five shots had killed the family, all at close range.

Prior to being killed Sheila had been treated for schizophrenia in a psychiatric hospital and suspicion fell on her to be the killer until Julie Mugford, Bamber's girlfriend told the police he had admitted to her that he did it. At his trial the prosecution argued that there was no evidence of the phone call Bamber said he had received from his father and that Nevill was too injured at the time to make any call, that there was no blood on the phone and that he would have called the police direct not phoning Bamber to do so. They also argued that the silencer was on the rifle when the shots were fired, a silencer is an extension to the barrel and that Sheila's hand would not have been able to reach the trigger and pull it if the rifle was held at her throat for a suicide shot. Her arm was not long enough. She had also been shot twice in the suicide which was not possible. The jury returned a majority verdict finding that Bamber had murdered the family to secure a large inheritance and then placed the rifle in his sister's hands to make the scene appear as a murder-suicide. He was given life imprisonment with a whole life tariff. He has unsuccessfully appealed the conviction in 2001, 2004, and 2012 having not identified any new evidence that might raise the possibility that his conviction was wrong.

He has made two unsuccessful attempts with lawsuits to claim a share of his family's estate. His grandmother cut him out of her will when he was arrested and most of the inheritance went to June Bamber's sister. He also tried unsuccessfully to claim part of the profits from the Maldon Caravan site.

He is a category A prisoner in HM Prison, Wakefield, Yorkshire where he helps other prisoners to read and write. He has an outside group of supporters who support his innocence and has developed several close relationships with women. He has been attacked twice in prison with one attack resulting in 28 stitches to a neck wound.

****

1985 JOHN DUFFY & DAVID MULCAHY

John Duffy and David Mulcahy met in a Haverstock, North London school as teenagers and shared a rather nasty, sadistic streak for injuring and killing animals which progressed as they got older culminating in killing women to satisfy their sexual fantasies. Duffy became the Railway Rapist striking at lone women at railway stations in South East, Western and Northern London. It was a good fifteen years after he was arrested and sentenced that it came to light he had an accomplice on the attacks, David Mulcahy although the police had long suspected it. It was the new forensic techniques that led to Mulcahy plus the first time use of Psychological Offender Profiling.

The pair left school and continued their close relationship as building site workers with Duffy then taking work as a carpenter on the railways and it is thought that they realised that railway stations were very quiet at night and an ideal place to attack and rape. It is known both were bullied at school and this way of establishing a command over another person to regain self esteem is often associated with sexual assaults on women. Whatever it was it grew inside them as they got older. Duffy actually married and took an interest in the martial arts. Their first crime was in Hampstead on1st July 1982 when they raped a twenty-three year old woman. Duffy was already known to the police for assaulting and raping his wife violently. After the first Hampstead attack eighteen more women were attacked over the next year and even more in 1984 with three being raped on the same night in Hendon in 1985. A police investigation called Operation Hart was launched.

Alison Day aged nineteen was followed off a train at Hackney Wick Station by Duffy and Mulcahy and grabbed, beaten and raped. She was then murdered by strangulation and thrown into the River Lea her clothes weighted down with stones. Prior to this the media had called the case 'Railway Rapist' now they changed it to 'Railway Killer' East London police set up a task force known as 'Operation Lea'. Two police forces were now looking for the pair.

Martye Tamboezer was just fifteen when she was raped and murdered by strangulation in West Horsley on 17th April 1986 and her dead body set on fire. Surrey police set up 'Operation Bluebell'. The Alison Day enquiry had been taken over by Detective Superintendent Charles Farquhar, a specialist east London murder investigator who linked Day's murder with the others when he looked at the Tamboezer crime scene photos and spotted that a belt and twig were similar to the Day ligature.

Anne Locke, a secretary was abducted and murdered after leaving a train at Brookhams Park Station in Hertfordshire on 18th May 1986. This resulted in a multi force task force being set up collating all three murders. It was the first time murder investigations had used computers and early use of the HOLMES program, Home Office Large Major Enquiry System. Duffy's name was identified as a suspect of interest and because of his previous assault and rape of his wife more attention was paid to him. A type of rope known as somyarn was found at his parents' home which linked him to the

Tamboezer murder. Mulcahy was also brought in for questioning and took an identity parade for the rape victims who had survived but was released as he was not clearly identified. Duffy had now started to rape alone and was arrested whilst following a potential victim in a park. He was questioned and then charged on all counts of rape and murder. He did not say anything about Mulcahy being his partner. He went to trial in February 1988 and was convicted of two murders and four rapes. He was acquitted of the murder of Anne Locke as her body had been in water for some time before being found and all DNA evidence had gone. He was sentenced to thirty years minimum later extended to whole life by the Home Secretary and then the European Court of Human Rights ruled it illegal for politicians to reset prison tariff and it reverted to the original 30 years.

This case extensively used psychological profiling which was being experimented with at the University of Surrey under Dr David Canter. The profiling of the Railway Killer fitted thirteen of the seventeen observations Canter had made about the killer and from then on became a serious part of all murder investigations.

In 1997 Duffy decided to implicate Mulcahy, then a married father of four. His once great friend had not visited him once in prison which had annoyed him. Police tracked Mulcahy for several months before arresting him. DNA tests were now in use and resulted in Mulcahy being convicted of three murders and seven rapes with Duffy as a prosecution witness. He was given three life sentences minimum 30 years. His own new evidence and cold case DNA tests then led to Duffy to being convicted of seventeen more rapes and having a further 12 years tagged onto his sentence. Neither will ever be released and police still suspect the pair of many more sex attacks taken place in the 1970s.

****

1986 MICHAEL LUPO

Michael Lupo was born on 19th January in Genzano di Lucania in Italy and travelled the world settling in England in 1975. He was gay and had an interest in sadomasochism and pursued that wherever he went always taking the dominant role.

He opened his own boutique catering for wealthy gay men who had found it a place to go and have sex with others of the same persuasion. Lupo took a very active and dominant role whenever he could. He moved to Roland Garden in South Kensington where he turned one room into a torture chamber to satisfy his sexual demands of others. He boasted about having sex with 4000+ men and picked many up in local gay bars. In 1986 unsurprisingly Lupo was diagnosed HIV positive which brought out an anger within him and within 2 months he murdered four gay men by strangulation. In each case he slashed open their bodies and smeared them with excrement, which became his calling card.

On 15th March 1986 James Burns a thirty-seven year old railway worker was found dead in a derelict property in Kensington, London. The investigation into his death faltered and was closed when no link between Burns and any possible killer was found. On 6th April 1986 the body of Anthony Connolly twenty-four was discovered on a railway embankment in Brixton, South London. His own scarf had been used to strangle him. Connolly was gay and shared a flat with another gay who was HIV positive.

After two very frightened young gay men came to the police with a story about a sadistic and strange man who had attempted to strangle them during sex Lupo was linked to the murders. On 18th May Michele del Marco Lupo was arrested at his home where he took police on a tour of the torture chamber whilst openly recounting the pleasure his killings had given him. He was charged with the murders of Burns and Connelly. The charge sheet was added to on May 21st with the murders of a young nurse Damien McClosky found strangled in West London and an unidentified male found near Hungerford Bridge over the Thames. In addition

Lupo was charged with two attempted murders. He admitted all and seemed to be seeking celebrity status wherever possible. He was sentenced to five terms of life imprisonment plus fourteen years at Frankland Prison, Durham where he died of AIDs related illness on February 12th 1995. He had been diagnosed HIV positive and knew he had little time left when sentenced. An international cold case review traced all the foreign places Lupo had visited to pick up men and found his favourites were Berlin, Hamburg, Los Angeles and New York. All places where mutilated bodies of gay men had been found over the period Lupo was there but no corpse was ever positively attributed to Lupo's actions. Most were decomposed too far when found.

****

1986 KENNETH ERSKINE

Born in Hammersmith, London on July 1st 1963 Kenneth Erskine, later to acquire the nickname 'The Stockwell Strangler' was one of three boys born to a British mother and Antiguan father. The parents divorced when he was twelve and Erskine was put in various homes and special schools.

Erskine became a drifter around London with no job and living on benefit payments and theft to feed his solvent abuse habit. In his early twenties he carried out his serial killing spree but his earlier house burglary crimes for which he served prison time had put his fingerprints on police files and he was quickly identified as the killer. The police had been clear by the MO in each murder that they were the work of one person. The usual entry point to the victim's house was through an unlocked ground floor window and in each case the killer had knelt on the victims chest with one hand over their mouth whilst the other was used to strangle them. Four of the victims had been sodomised before or after death.

Erskine's first victim was Nancy Elms 78 of Wandsworth, murdered on 9th April 1986. The doctor had issued a death certificate for Elms stating 'natural causes' and only when her home help noticed that the television was missing from Elm's flat did the police act. A post mortem was called for and it found Elms had been raped and strangled.

Next on Erskine's list was Janet Cockett 67, killed on 9th June 1986 in Wandsworth. He strangled her in her council flat on the estate where she was Chairwoman of the Tenant's association. Again natural causes was originally put as the reason for her death but a post mortem showed she had been murdered but not sexually assaulted. The forensic examination of Cockett's flat revealed Erskine's palm print on the window sill.

Two Polish men were Erskine's next victims. On 28th June 1986 he sexually assaulted and strangled Valentine Gleim 84 and Zbigniew Strabawa 94 after getting into their residential home in Stockwell.

On the 8th July 1986 he broke into 84 year old William Carmen's flat in Islington, stole some money and then molested and strangled him.

On 21st July 1986 he repeated the same MO at 74 year old William Downe's bedsit in Stockwell.

The last of Erskine's victims was Florence Tisdall 83 who he raped and strangled on 23rd July 1986 at her flat in Ranelagh Gardens Mansions in Fulham.

Police were looking for Erskine by now after finding the palm print he left at Cockett's flat and they found him in a homeless hostel and pulled him in for interviewing. Pretty sure he was the killer they put him in a line-up and 74 year old Fred Prentice who had claimed Erskine had broken into his flat and tried to strangle him a month previously was able to identify him. Although Erskine was strongly suspected of four other murders including Wilfred Parkes 81 killed in Stockwell on June 2nd 1986 and Trevor Thomas 75 strangled at Lambeth on 21st July 1986 not enough evidence was found to go forward with any charges.

Found guilty of seven murders in January 1988 Erskine was sentenced to life imprisonment with a recommended 40 year tariff. He was found to have mental disorders of chronic schizophrenia and antisocial personality and transferred from prison to Broadmoor Hospital and at the time of writing is still there and unlikely to be freed before 2028. In 2009 an appeal against the murder convictions using the mental health act had his conviction reduced to manslaughter on the grounds of diminished responsibility.

An interesting aside is that Erskine and another convicted murderer inmate at Broadmoor, Jamie Devitt, successfully saved the life of serial killer Peter Sutcliffe when he was attacked in his room at Broadmoor Hospital's Henley ward by Paul Wilson who attempted to strangle Sutcliffe with the flex from a pair of headphones.

****

1987 STEPHEN GRIFFITHS

Stephen Shaun Griffiths was born on Xmas Eve 1969, the eldest of three children of Stephen Griffiths, salesman, and Moira Dewhirst a telephonist and confidence trickster who would be later convicted of benefit fraud. The couple split and divorced when young Stephen was thirteen and he stayed with his mother in their council house. He had a habit of watching his mother whilst she had sex with numerous men friends. He soon accumulated a criminal record for shoplifting and at one theft when aged seventeen he attacked a clerk who tried to apprehend him cutting the clerk's face with a knife. He was sentenced to three years youth custody for this. In prison he lost contact with his family and boasted about wanting to be a serial killer to his psychiatrists. Upon his release he lived in a flat in Holmfield Court, Manningham, Bradford close to Thornton Road a well known red light area from where Griffiths will pluck three of them to be victims. At this time he enrolled in a psychology course at Bradford College. In 1989 he was given 100 hours of community work after shooting birds which he then dissected. The following year he was again arrested for threatening a girl who rejected his advances and holding a knife to her throat. His interest in serial killers surfaced when he was released and collected as many books on them as he could afford. He showed particular interest in the Yorkshire Ripper. He dated a woman for two years but she ended it when she found he had covered every surface in his flat with plastic and knew about his fascination with murder. His next regular girlfriend ended their relationship when he became violent and abusive. He then stalked and harassed her for two years disappearing when the police were called and arrived.

In 2001 Griffiths started going off the rails, taking drugs and drinking heavily. He bought two large lizards that he took for walks on dog leads and his neighbour Rachel Farrington witnessed him feeding live rats to the lizards whilst another neighbour William Parkin saw Griffiths eat a live baby rat himself. In 2003 he earned a Bachelor's Degree in Psychology and enrolled in the University of Bradford on a Ph.D course the following year. Being unemployed and living on benefit and grants he spent his time on the internet viewing violent pornography and quoting fictional killers on his MySpace account which bore his user name of 'Ven Pariah' a fictional demon.

The need to kill began to usurp his every thought and he decided rationally to become a serial killer of sex workers in the Bradford area as a tribute to Peter Sutcliffe who had killed some of his victims in the same area. On 22nd June 2009 Griffith's picked up sex worker Susan Rushworth and took her to his flat where he killed her and dismembered her body in the bath. He killed another two victims in the following twelve months. His second victim was Shelley Armitage 31 murdered on April 26th. On the 21st May his third and final victim Suzanne Blamires tried to escape but was shot with a crossbow (Griffiths had two) and then stabbed to death. This was caught on CCTV in the hallway of the flats where he lived and led to his arrest. On trial Griffiths would refer to himself with a certain amount of pride as 'the crossbow cannibal', this stemmed from his modus operandi which was to roam the red light district of Bradford and persuade a sex worker to come back with him to his flat and kill them, most likely by tying them up and shooting them with one of his crossbows. He would then dismember them in his bath and cook parts of the bodies to eat. Parts he didn't eat were put inside plastic bags and dumped in a nearby lake.

Police suspect Griffiths of other murders but cannot produce enough good evidence to take to court. 1992 September 12th Yvonne Fitt 33 found bound and stabbed at Northwood Edge, Caldy; 1994 May, Dawn Shield 19, found strangled in Derbyshire, East Midlands; May 2000 Gemma Simpson 24 missing from Leeds, Yorkshire; 2001 April 26th Rebecca Hall 19 bludgeoned to death; November 2001 Michaela Hague 25, stabbed to death. He is also suspected of killing at least three more women.

****

1988 ANTHONY ARKWRIGHT.

Arkwright went on a murdering rampage in August 1988 and killed three people in Wath-upon-Dearne, Yorkshire over just 56 hours. He is also suspected of killing a fourth person, this charge still lays open on file.

Arkwright was born in 1967 in the mining town of Wath-upon-Deane as one of five siblings. His father was a miner like most of the town's men and his mother walked out on the family when he was very young. Local rumours were that he was the issue of his mother's incestuous relationship with his grandfather and although untrue the stigma attached to that drove her away. He spent the vast majority of his childhood in care and care homes and greatly under achieved at various schools whilst committing petty crimes on a regular basis. When he was 21 he was working at a scrap yard but his poor attendance led to him being sacked on the 27th August 1988 and his killings began.

His first victim was his own grandfather, 68-year-old Lithuanian born Stanislav Pudoikas who was tending his allotment on Ruskin Drive, Mexborough, he stabbed Pudoikas before dragging the still alive body into an allotment shed and crushing his skull with a 7kg lump hammer and axe. Arkwright then went on a pub crawl in Mexborough and as the beer took effect said things about the murder but without admitting anything, things like ' It's been bloody murder on my grand-dad's allotment today' and expressing his interest in becoming better known than the Yorkshire Ripper. Arkwright went to his grandfather's house and was intent on stealing his grandfather's £3000 savings when caught in the act by Pudoikas's housekeeper, 73 year old Elsa Kronadaite who he killed. Next was Arwright's neighbour, Raymond Ford an unemployed teacher who Arwright continually bullied and stole from. Ford had already reported the thefts to the police and fuelled by drink and the power that murdering two people and seemingly having got away with it had given him Arwright sought revenge for Ford reporting him. At 3am in the morning of the 28th August 1988 he broke into Ford's flat naked except for a devil mask and stabbed Ford two hundred and fifty times and scattered Ford's entrails around the room. He then left and went home, showered and answered the door at 7am to the police who had come to arrest him for stealing from Ford. They were unaware Ford lay dismembered in his flat next door. Arkwright was interviewed for three hours and then released on police bail with a court appearance scheduled for the following week. He went on another drinking spree to celebrate being a murderer and being released by the police. The next day Arkwright broke into the disability adapted bungalow belonging to his other next door neighbour, Marcus Law who was twenty-five and wheelchair bound after a motorbike accident. He stabbed Law more than seventy times before trying to removed his innards, when this failed he pushed one of Law's crutches deep into the open wound and gouged out Law's eyes inserting cigarettes into the eye sockets, ears and mouth. Later in custody he described this murder as punishment for Law for all the cigarettes he'd scrounged off Arkwright. As he left Law's bungalow he passed Law's mother coming to do some cleaning and remarked how sorry he was to hear of Law's suicide. Law's mother found her son's body. The police immediately arrested Arkwright and only when he was questioned at the police station and confessed to four murders did they realise they had a serial killer in custody and began a search for the other bodies which they quickly found. Arkwright invented a false fifth victim which led to fruitless search of waterways and lakes in the area. He was remanded to HMP Hull and after convincing the prison doctor he was insane by daubing excrement around his cell and demanding to be treated as a hero for what he'd done he was transferred to Rampton Secure Psychiatric Hospital in Nottinghamshire where the psychiatrists there gave the opinion he was sane with one even writing that he was the 'sanest person in the building, including the doctors'

He was found guilty in Sheffield Crown Court in July 1989, he had pleaded guilty and was sentenced to life imprisonment. The murder of Kronadaite was unproven and the judge ordered it to lie on file. His term was changed to whole life with no parole by The Home Secretary David Blunkett in 2003. This was challenged by the EU Court of Human Rights but failed. Arkwright together with another killer, Arthur Hutchinson appealed against their whole life tariffs in February 2014 but three High Court Judges rejected the appeals.

****

1990 STEVEN GRIEVESON

Steven Grieveson became known as the Sunderland Strangler and murdered 4 boys between 1990 and 1994 in Sunderland. Grieveson was born on December 14th 1970 and not a lot is known about his early years or schooling except that he has convictions going back to the age of 11 and had amassed twenty-five convictions by the time of his trial. After he left school he took various jobs on fairgrounds where he could pick up young boys for homosexual acts.

On 26th November 1993 he killed Thomas Kelly 18 in an old tumble down allotment shed in Fulwell, Sunderland by strangulation and set the body on fire. On February 4th 1994 he killed and set fire to David Hanson 15, in Roker Terrace where he lived and then on 25th February 1994 murdered David Grieff on the abandoned allotment where he had killed Thomas Kelly three months earlier. Strangulation was used in all the killings.

All three victims were pupils at Monkwearmouth Academy which led police at the time to think that the murderer maybe a present or past pupil at the academy. Grieveson had in fact attended Hylton Red House School.

On 11th March 1994 Grieveson was charged with attempted burglary at Roker Terrace at the same house that the burnt body of David Hanson had been found. The subsequent police investigation tied Grieveson to the murder and to those of Grieff and Kelly. At trial it was revealed that all three murders were committed after Grieveson had had homosexual relations with the deceased, either by consent or by force, and set the bodies alight to conceal this. He was charged with the three murders in November 1995, found guilty and given three life sentences with a minimum 35 year tariff.

In November 2000 following further police cold case enquiries Grieveson was questioned at Full Sutton Prison about the May 1990 murder of fourteen year old Simon Martin, killed at Gilside House, Roker. Grieveson denied he had anything to do with it and no charges were brought, further enquiries over the next years and new forms of forensic tests were deemed to offer enough substantial evidence to charge him on 22nd November 2012 and he admitted being responsible on the 11th February 2013. He was convicted at Newcastle Crown Court on 24th October 2013. As far as we know at the time of writing he is in HMP Full Sutton maximum security prison in East Riding, Yorkshire.

****

1991 BEVERLEY ALLITT

Beverley Allitt, born 4th October 1968, was one of four children and grew up in the village of Corby Glen near Grantham. She left school at 15 and enrolled on a course in nursing at Grantham College. She became a State Enrolled Nurse at Grantham and Kesteven Hospital in Lincolnshire and during a period of fifty-nine days between February and April in 1991 whilst working on the Children's Ward murdered four children, attempted to murder another five and inflicted 'Grevious Bodily Harm' on a further six. It is unknown how Allitt killed all the victims but a large air bubble was found in the blood stream of one and another two are suspected of having large doses of insulin injected into them.

The victims were; Liam Taylor 7 weeks old murdered on 22nd February 1991; Timothy Hardwick 11 years old murdered on 5th March 1991; Rebecca Phillips 2 months old murdered 3rd April 1991; Claire Peck 15 months old; Kayley Desmond 1 year old attacked on 8th March 1991 but resuscitated on the ward and transferred to another hospital and recovered; Paul Crampton 5 months old, Allitt injected him 3 times with insulin overdoses on the day he was transferred to another hospital where he survived; Bradely Gibson 5 years old had two cardiac arrests after Allitt gave him insulin overdoses but survived and transferred; Michael Davidson 6 years old, admitted for an operation and injected with insulin many times through a cannula on his hand by Allitt, he fell unconscious but was stabilised by other doctors on the ward and made a full recovery; Yik Hung Chan, 2 years old, Allitt restricted his oxygen and he was transferred and survived; Katie Phillips 2 months old, the twin of Rebecca Phillips admitted as a precaution after Rebecca's death. She suffered two unexplained apnoeic episodes and was transferred to another hospital after the second one but it resulted in permanent brain damage, partial paralysis and blindness due to oxygen deprivation. Unbelievably her parents were so grateful for Allitt's care of Rebecca they asked her to be Katie's Godmother. In 1999 Katie was awarded £2,2125m by Lincolnshire

Health Authority to cover the cost of treatment and care for the rest of her life.

It was after the death of Rebecca that medical staff became suspicious of the high number of cardiac arrests on the children's ward and called in the police. A process of elimination and computer record analysis showed that Allitt was the sole nurse on duty at the time of all the attacks with access to the drugs. She was arrested and charged with four counts of murder, eleven counts of attempted murder and eleven counts of GBH. In May 1993 she stood trial at Nottingham Crown Court and pleaded not guilty to all the charges and on 28th May 1993 was found guilty of all charges and sentenced to thirteen concurrent terms of life imprisonment which, at the time of writing, she is serving at Rampton Secure Hospital in Nottinghamshire

Several reasons for Allitt's behaviour have been floated and the one experts think most likely is that she suffers from *factitious disorder* also known as Munchausen Syndrome where a person causes

harm to others in their care in order bring attention
on themselves.

****

1991 PETER TOBIN

Peter Britton Tobin born 27th August 1946 in Johnstone, Renfrewshire was one of eight children having four older sisters and three younger brothers. He was sent to an approved school aged just seven and later served time in borstals before being convicted of burglary and forgery in 1970 and sent to prison. In 1969 he moved to Brighton, Sussex where he married seventeen year old Margaret Mountney. They separated after just one year and divorced in 1971. In 1973 Tobin married again, this time to a local nurse Sylvia Jefferies age thirty with whom he had a son and daughter. The marriage was violent and ended in 1976 when Sylvia left with their son. Tobin then had a son with his new girlfriend Cathy Wilson after they married in 1987. They moved to Bathgate in Scotland in 1990 and shortly after Wilson left Tobin and moved back to Portsmouth, Hampshire, the city she had grown up in. All three wives later said Tobin initially presented a loving and caring attitude which quickly turned sadistic and violent during their marriages.

The first recorded attack by Tobin was on 4th August 1993 when he sexually assaulted and raped two fourteen year old school girls who were visiting a friend in the next door flat. She was out and Tobin asked if they would like to wait in his flat. Once inside he held them at knife point and plied them with cider and vodka before the assaults which were witnessed by his young son. He then turned on the gas and left them to die. They survived and Tobin disappeared surfacing in Coventry where he joined a religious sect the Jesus Fellowship under a false name claiming homelessness. He moved to Brighton and was arrested soon after when his car was found there. The police had his number plate registration and knew it was a blue colour. Tobin pleaded guilty at Winchester Court to the assaults and attempted murder of the two girls and was sent down for fourteen years being released in 2004. Now 58 he returned to Paisley in Renfrewshire where he assumed the name Pat McLaughlin as his real name was now on the Sex Offender's Register. There was an arrest warrant out for him because he had moved there without notifying the police of a change of address. He managed to get a job as a handyman at St Patrick's Church in Anderston, Glasgow.

Angelika Kluk was a twenty-three year old Polish student was staying at the presbytery of St Patrick's and worked as a cleaner. She was last seen in Tobin's company on 24th September 2006. Police found her body on 29th September stuffed in an underground chamber under the floorboards of the Church near the Church Confessional. She had been beaten, raped and stabbed and forensic evidence pointed to her being alive when put beneath the floorboards. Tobin fled but was arrested in London quite soon after as he had tried to get admitted into hospital with a false complaint and false name. At The Edinburgh High Court Tobin was found guilty of the rape and murder of Kluk and sentenced to life imprisonment with a minimum tariff of 21 years.

After this the Lothian and Borders Police re-opened a cold case into the murder of Vicky Hamilton a fifteen year old girl who disappeared in Bathgate on 10th February 1991. Tobin had a house and lived in Bathgate at that time. Hamilton was last seen waiting for a bus home to Redding near Falkirk but never arrived home or got on any bus. Tobin left Bathgate and went to live in Margate a few days after. The old Bathgate house was searched as was the Margate property at 50 Irvine Drive. Human remains found in the garden at Margate were identified as those of Vicky Hamilton. Tobin was tried for the Hamilton's murder in November 2008 at the High Court Dundee. The evidence was circumstantial plus forensic of DNA and fingerprints left on a knife at his former house, on Hamilton's purse and the sheeting in which her body had been wrapped. Tobin was found guilty on 2nd December 2008 and received another life sentence.

On 16th November 2007 a second body was found at 50 Irvine Drive, Margate and confirmed to be that of eighteen year old Dinah McNicol from Tillingham, Essex. She was last seen alive whilst hitchhiking home with a male friend from a music festival in Liphook. The friend left the car at Junction 8 of the M25 leaving McNicol in the car with the driver, she was never seen again. Her credit card was used at several ATMs in Hampshire and Sussex until police put a stop on it at her family's request. Essex police re-opened the case in 2007 after 'receiving new evidence' which was probably the result of things coming out in the Kluk case. The CPS served a summons on Tobin in jail via his solicitors and after being delayed whilst Tobin had surgery it took place at Chelmsford Crown court on 16th December and the jury gave a guilty verdict and the judge gave Tobin his third life sentence.

A nationwide police investigation named Operation Anagram looking into the possibility of Tobin having committed more murders was started after his first conviction in 2006. Police forces could see similarities in unsolved murder cases and disappearances of young girls on their files with Tobin's MO. After the McNicol trial Anagram was re-activated and looked deeply into Tobin's past movements and his possible involvement in thirteen other unsolved murders including three of an unidentified killer called Bible John. Tobin made boasts in prison during his time there of killing forty-eight people. Anagram failed to identify any further victims with enough factual or forensic evidence to go to court with and wound down in 2011 although it still remains active.

Bible John is a serial killer who murdered three girls in Glasgow in 1960s. The similarities occur between photos of Tobin at that time in his life and artist sketches made from eyewitness reports of Bible John which included a missing front tooth which Tobin also had. Tobin's exit from Scotland happened at the same time that the Bible John killings ceased. Although the cases are ongoing it is not likely to yield a killer as the DNA evidence has deteriorated because of the poor storage facilities that it has been kept in.

****

1992 ROBERT NAPPER

The eldest of four children of Brian Napper, a driving instructor, and his wife Pauline, Robert was born on 25th February 1966 in Erith, South East London and brought up in Plumstead. His parents had a violent relationship with attacks on his mother being witnessed by the young boy. They divorced when he was nine and the children were put into foster care and given psychiatric treatment and counselling at Maudsley Hospital in Camberwell. Napper's counselling lasted 6 years. Napper had Asperger's syndrome and paranoid schizophrenia which was not know at the time and resulted in him being socially aggressive at school. He was sexually assaulted on a camping holiday with the offender being jailed which brought about a change in Napper as he became introverted and reclusive, bullying his siblings and spying on his sister while she was naked bathing.

Robert Napper's first offence was with an airgun in 1986 for which he was convicted by the police and fined for carrying a firearm. In October

1989 his mother told the police that Napper had told her he had raped a woman on Plumstead Common. Nothing in the police files matched this admission at the time but it emerged after his second conviction that a 30 year old woman had indeed been raped, in front of her children in her house that backed onto Plumstead common at the time Napper had told his mother of the rape. Pauline Napper broke off all contact with her son at this point. His second victim and first murder victim was Rachel Nickell who he attacked, killed and then sexually assaulted in a secluded part of Wimbledon Common on 15th July 1992 in front of her two year old son. He stabbed her forty-nine times. He was questioned and eliminated and another man, Colin Stagg was wrongly charged after a police 'honeytrap' sting. Stagg was later acquitted with the Judge throwing the case out and reprimanding the police for the tactics they used on 'trapping' Stagg. The Colin Stagg story is very interesting with him finally receiving £706,000 compensation for wrongful arrest and after serving 14 months on remand, but out of the remit of this book.

As we will see later in this piece Napper was finally charged and convicted of Nickell's murder later in 2002 with the use of new and advanced forensic techniques when a cold case review enquiry was opened.

In November 1993 Napper stabbed Samantha Bisset in her home in Plumstead killing her and then sexually assaulted her four year old daughter Jazmima Bisset before smothering her, positioning her as though asleep in bed and placing her toys around her. Napper than dismembered Samantha's body and took with him various parts as 'trophies'. Napper's fingerprint was found at Bisset's flat and he was arrested. In May 1994 he was charged with their murders and convicted at the Old Bailey in October 1995. He also admitted to two rapes and attempted rapes at this time.

Napper is also the most likely person to be the 'Green Chain Rapist' the name given to a man who carried out at least eighty-six rape attacks in South East London from 1990 to 1994. The Green Chain being a series of leafy and open spaces between the

Thames and Crystal Palace Park created by the London Borough Councils and called the Green Chain Walk. Napper admitted in the Bisset interviews to two rapes and two attempted rapes in the Green Chain which he kept notes about but he is suspected of many more. He is known to have attempted to rape two seventeen year old girls one week apart in March 1992 in the Green Chain and in May successfully raped a twenty two year old woman there as well.

He is at the time of writing still in Broadmoor Maximum Security prison.

****

1993 COLIN IRELAND

Known as the Gay Slayer Colin Ireland send shivers of fear amongst the gay community in the early 1990s. Abused by paedophiles as a young boy he sought vengeance to abate the anger within him. Ireland was not gay himself and had been married. His mother, a shop assistant, had him at a young age of sixteen and had various partners that she brought into the house during his younger life. Colin was born on 16th March 1954 in Dartford, Kent and pretty soon after his father left his mother. He doesn't to this day know his father's name as his mother didn't put it on the birth certificate and never told him. He spent the first five years with his mother's parents as she moved back in with them before moving to Kent with a new partner that soon broke down. In the next six years mother and son moved nine times including stints in homeless refuges which Ireland later described as 'degradation personified'. His mother was unskilled and badly educated and her parents persuaded her to move back in with them. In 1961 his mother had a new partner and the three of them moved to Dartford where she married this partner. He was an electrician and treated Colin well but his work was mainly temporary on building sites and the family were poor. Ireland attended five schools and was bullied because he was bow legged and thin. He avoided going to school whenever he could and suffered the cane on many occasions for repeated lateness and none attendance. In 1964 with Ireland aged ten the family was evicted and his mother was again pregnant and couldn't afford to keep him and so placed him in care taking him back when a new home was found. The stepfather left soon after and in 1966 his mother remarried. Colin was twelve and refused to take the new man's surname and reverted to Ireland. This stepfather gave Ireland the only stability he had as a young man. Ireland was first approached for sex with a man whilst working at a fairground in his school summer holidays, he was offered a necklace for his mother in exchange for a sexual act. Other offers followed, Ireland was twelve and was asked to performed sexual acts with men in public toilets, at the cinema, at a second hand shop and even his optician propositioned him. Ireland says he refused each time and grew more and more angry, the anger built up in his mind. He was gaining a police record for theft, burglary and blackmail in his teens with two sessions in a Borstal and at twenty-one was sentenced to 18 months in prison. He served 12 months in London and was then transferred to Lewes prison to complete the sentence. He was released in November 1976 and went to live in Swindon where he met and married a black West Indian woman, she was five years older than him and already with 4 children. They lived together and Ireland says they planned to marry but never did. In 1977 he was found guilty of 'demanding money with menace' and sentenced to eighteen months, in 1980 he got two years for robbery, in1981 two months for deception and in 1985 six months for 'going equipped to rob.' He tried to join and was rejected by the army and began to dress in para-military clothes and often camped out on the Essex moors at night. He was twice married. He was working as a chef when he met and married Virginia Zammit in 1981. She was thirty-six, nine years his senior with a five year old daughter and wheelchair bound after a car accident left her partially paralysed at twenty-four. They married in 1982 and lived on a housing estate in Holloway where he was known as 'the gentle giant' to the neighbours. He was soon back in prison and the couple divorced in 1987. In 1989 he met Janet Young the landlady of the Globe pub in Buckfast, Devon and moved in with her and her two children living above the pub within a week of meeting her. They married at Newton Abbot Registry Office and after a few months of marriage Ireland took his wife and children to meet his mother in Margate and whilst there stole Young's car, plundered her business bank account and disappeared. They divorced and he took various jobs in various places and even worked in a homeless shelter in London for a time before being sacked for violent behaviour. He made a conscious decision to be a serial murderer. He moved to Southend and was aware that Geographic Profiling of a killer usually points to his killing area being within a tight radius of his home, so he made a decision to kill in London forty two miles away.

He selected gay men as his target as he thought they would be easy to lure into his home and more likely to agree to bondage with a stranger. In 1993 his first victim was Peter Walker a 45 year old theatre choreographer that Ireland picked up in a London gay bar called The Coleherne. The bar in the Brompton road was well known within the gay community and customers would wear colour-coded handkerchiefs indicating their preferred sexual activity which made picking up similar minded individuals easy. Ireland colour-coded to be a 'dominant S&M partner' and attracted Walker. They went to Walker's flat where Ireland tied the naked Walker to his bed, whipped him and killed him with a plastic bag over the head. Ireland left the body with condoms in the mouth and the body itself arranged on the bed in a sexual position with Walker's teddy bears. He thoroughly cleaned the flat and disposed of any items that could lead back to him. He then stayed the night at Walker's flat and travelled home the next morning in the rush hour. Two days later Ireland phoned the Samaritans to tell them where he had put Walker's dogs which he had locked in a separate room with food and water and then he called the Sun newspaper directing them to the flat and admitting the murder.

The police had no clues and the autopsy couldn't say whether Walker's death was accidental of murder as sadomasochistic sex between consenting adults was a legal sexual pursuit.

In May Ireland went back to the Coleherne bar and picked up Christopher Dunn, a thirty-seven year old librarian. Dunn's body was found nude, gagged and bound his testicles burnt with a gas lighter in his north east London home on May 30th and was recorded as a possible accident. No link to Walker's death three months earlier was made or suspected. Within a week this theory was dashed as Ireland used Dunn's bank card to withdraw £200 from an ATM and called the police anonymously to rebuke them for their failure to link the two crimes. Dunn's money was used to buy new gloves and shoes, Ireland had read a lot about serial killing and knew he had to have new shoes and gloves each time but being unemployed on benefit he could not afford them on his weekly payment.

On June 7th the body of an American, Perry Bradley III, a closet homosexual was found in his Kensington apartment. He was naked and bound, strangled with a plastic sex doll arranged on his body in a sexual position. His credit cards were missing and £200 was withdrawn at an ATM. Ireland phoned the police several days late and told them, 'I did the American, I left clues at the scene for you to find me' The detectives found no clues as Ireland had once again cleaned the flat, but they were more worried as Ireland had also told them of his desire to be a serial killer and that having read the FBI's book on serial killing available at UK libraries he 'knew how many I have to kill to be called serial killer'. He also told them later after his arrest that at the time of Perry's murder he was 'speeding up and couldn't stop' His next anonymous call to the police after Perry's murder was almost a plea for them to catch him and berated them for not linking the three murders.

On June 7th Ireland was back at the Colherne Bar picking up thirty-three year old Andrew Collier. At Collier's flat he tied him to the bed, handcuffed and strangled him. He then strangled Collier's cat and positioned it onto the body with its mouth round Collier's penis and its tail in his mouth. He cleaned the crime scene up with a towel but missed one fingerprint on a window frame.

A few days later on June 15th he met Emanuel Spiteri, a chef and once back at Spiteri's flat bound and strangled him. He set fire to the flat before he left but the fire didn't take hold and went out. The crime hadn't been found or reported when Ireland phoned the police the next day to ask them 'have you found the body and the fire yet?'

The police now had to admit they had a serial killer at large in London and before they could make a scheduled press announcement he rang again, 'The FBI classify a serial killer as having killed 4 people, I have done 5 so I may stop now. I just wanted to see if it could be done, I will probably not reoffend again.'

Scotland Yard took out all the stops and launched a massive publicity campaign urging the killer to give himself up. They even handed out flyers at the Gay Pride Festival. They learnt that Spiteri had travelled by train to Catford with another man on the night he was killed and the station CCTV camera gave a poor picture of the two men, Spiteri and a large, heavy built man. The photos were published and over four hundred gay men reported seeing him in the Coleherne Bar and talking with the 'big man'

A surprise move was made by Ireland on July 19th 1993 when he approached his solicitor admitting he was the man in the photo and claiming that Spiteri had been alive at his home together with another man and they had left together. Shown the evidence of his fingerprint at the Collier murder scene he finally admitted all five murders on August 19th.

He was sentenced to five life sentences. Rumour has it that he advanced it to six whilst in Wakefield prison where he strangled a cellmate, a convicted child-killer, no charges are listed as being filed against him, if the action is true, then because he was already serving life without parole and no harsher penalty is available what would be the point? It has been noted that soon after the reported killing Ireland was moved to a maximum security wing at Whitemoor Prison in Cambridgeshire to a single occupant cell.

Ireland is mentioned in the song 'Pain' by the Manic Street Preachers but no book has been written about him nor any substantial articles written or documentaries made at the time of writing this.

****

1995 PETER MOORE.

Peter Moore ran a chain of cinemas in Bagillt, Holyhead, Kimmel Bay and Denbigh plus a theatre in North Wales. He had a fixation with Jason Voorhies from the 'Friday the 13th' film series and mutilated and murdered four men near Welsh country towns in 1995. Moore was born in 1940 and did his killings between September and December 1995 dressed all in black which gave him the nickname 'The Man in Black'.

His first victim was Henry Roberts, fifty-six who Moore stabbed to death at Robert's home in Anglesey. Victim number two was Edward Carthy stabbed and then buried in a Clocaenog Forest after being tapped up by Moore in a gay bar. Number three was Keith Randles aged forty-nine, killed whilst sleeping in his works caravan at road works on the A5 in Anglesey. Moore told the police that Randles had asked why he was being stabbed and Moore told him 'for fun', later telling police that he 'enjoyed killing people'. This may have been a ruse to get himself certified as insane and face a lesser charge of manslaughter rather than murder. In December 1995 Moore's last victim was Tony Davies aged forty, a married father of two who was stabbed to death at a Pensarm beach near Abergele on the north Wales coast.

Moore came to the attention of the murder squad when an anonymous tip from a member of the public linked his van to one seen at the Anthony Davies murder scene, Pensarm Beach. Further forensic tests at the scene revealed Moore's blood on pebbles together with that of Davies. Searches of Moore's house turned up some of the various murder victims' clothes sunk into his garden pond along with a knife in a bag bearing all four victims blood traces. Nazi uniforms and memorabilia plus a real North Wales Police Sergeant's uniform and truncheon which he wore to 'scare them a little bit' were also found. The source of the police uniform was never established. Henry Robert's his first victim, was also interested in Nazi memorabilia.

At his trial in Mold Crown Court in 1996 Moore was accused of sexually attacking forty other men in twenty years of terror in North Wales and Merseyside which escalated to murder at the end. He insisted he was innocent and his gay lover 'Jason' the name of the killer in the Friday the 13th films was responsible. No trace of a 'lover' was ever found. He was given four full tariff life sentences. In 2012 he lost an appeal to the European Court against the 'whole life tariff.' During his time in Wakefield jail he became great friends with Harold Shipman who hanged himself in 2004. Several media outlets wrongly reported his death in jail in 2004 but at the time of writing he is still in Broadmoor.

****

1997 DAVID MOOR

Not to be mixed up with Peter Moore, the previous chapter. Whether David Moor was a serial killer or not is debateable. Moor worked as a GP in Stamfordham, Northumberland. His patient George Liddell 85, suffered from cancer of the bowel. After an operation to remove some of the cancerous tissues Liddell was sent home to be with his daughter and under the care of Moor and a team of nurses. Liddell's health deteriorated greatly and Moor prescribed 5mg diamorphine to be injected at intervals. This was doubled as Liddell's pain increased. His carers agreed he was terminally ill and told his daughter what to expect. He was transferred into a hospice and Moor upped the diamorphine to 30mg every 24 hours. Liddell got worse and on 19th July 1997 Moor injected diamorphine and chlorpromazine and Liddell passed away within twenty minutes. The whole episode would have passed without comment had the Sunday Times not carried an article on euthanasia and a journalist asked Moor for his views on the subject. Rather stupidly

Moor told her, on the record, that he had probably helped ten patients a year over 30 years to pain free release from their illnesses. This sparked an outrage with Moor being labelled 'Doctor Death' and 'Britain's greatest Serial Killer' by the tabloid press.

Moor was sent to trial at Newcastle Crown Court on April 4th 1999. The jury acquitted him after just 65 minutes of deliberation.

NOTE

There have been other doctors accused in similar circumstances and acquitted but the author feels they are outside the scope of this book.

****

2002 COLIN NORRIS

Norris was born on 12th February 1976 in Milton, Glasgow and seems to have had a normal early life at home and in education achieving an average academic record. On leaving education he worked at a travel agents and then decided to retrain as a nurse at the University of Dundee where he built a bit of a reputation for being quick tempered and warned about his behaviour which was deemed 'unacceptable'. He qualified in June 2001 and began working at Leeds General Infirmary but became awkward when nursing elderly patients refusing to change their bedding or clothes. He would avoid placements at nursing homes and feigned illness in order not to attend them telling other nurses that he hated geriatric people. He was caught stealing drugs from the hospital and somehow was not dismissed. Further suspicions about Norris were raised when he worked at the Leeds General Infirmary and the St James's University Hospital, Leeds and predicted the death of Ethel Hall, an elderly patient to a colleague saying 'I predict Ethel Hall will become unwell at

5.15 am.' She did, despite having no medical reason for an impending illness. She died a few weeks later. When she first became ill Norris was one of the nurses who attended to her and told the nurse that he had predicted her illness, 'I told you so' he said in a very arrogant way. Later when the police questioned Norris about Ethel Hall and three other patients who had unexpectedly passed away on his shift he told them, 'I seem to be unlucky for them.' The four who died were 79, 80, 86 and 88 years old. The police investigated a further seventy-two deaths that occurred on Norris's watch, although in some he was not the only nurse on duty. The investigations were conducted by an independent panel of experts who identified the three dead women as being the victims of a lethal injection of insulin. They also identified two others, one who died and one who survived a massive injection of insulin. Ethel Hall's blood contained a massive 1000 units of insulin in just one small sample and the expert who did the test said this was 12 times above the normal level. The only nurse that had been with the five dead patients within the previous two hours of them becoming terminally ill was Norris. The hospital's personnel shift records substantiated this and ruled out all other staff members.

The first victim was Vera Wilby who was in hospital for a broken hip and who Norris injected with morphine and then a mix of other drugs before he went off shift on May 17th 2002. An hour after he had gone off shift other nurses found Wilby semi-conscious. Their quick treatment saved her life. On June 12th Doris Ludlam was admitted with a broken hip and on the 25th Norris injected her with an unnecessary amount of mixed pain killers plus drugs to reduce blood sugar and then he went off shift. She was discovered in a coma forty minutes later. Another lady with a broken hip, eighty-eight year old Bridget Bourke was admitted on 16th June and discovered at 3.10am on 21st July suffering with an inexplicable hypoglycaemic attack which killed her. On October 10th Irene Crooks seventy-nine, was admitted with a broken hip and Norris recorded in the daily log that her condition was improving and then found her 'unresponsive' at 6am on 19th October having suffered a hypoglycaemic attack. She died the next day. A colleague later stated that Norris made no attempt to revive Crooks from her coma. None of these women plus Ethel Hall were diabetic and all were in hospital for a simple hip operation. The mistreatment of other elderly patients by Norris surfaced in the police enquiries. When an elderly man had asked Norris to empty his catheter bag the request had been refused and the patient told to do it himself and Norris went off duty. The patient fell on the way to the bathroom and lodged a report. Norris made his dislike of elderly people plainly obvious in the nasty and callous way he talked to them and wished they ' rot in hell'

Norris was sent to stand trial in March 2008 for the murder of the women and the attempted murder of one other. The jury took 4 days to bring in verdicts of guilty on all counts and on 3rd March 2008 he was sentenced to life imprisonment with a minimum tariff of 30 years. He was subsequently struck off The Nursing and Midwifery Council list.

One possible inspiration for Norris's behaviour was that he attended a talk at University about Jessie McTavish, a nurse who was eventually cleared of murdering an eighty year old patient in 1974 and had used the same procedures as Norris.

In 2010 an independent inquiry into Norris's murders recommended the introduction of 'student passports' which would monitor the personality traits and integrity of nursing students throughout their training. The idea behind this was that it may have flagged up that Norris had issues with the elderly before going into professional nursing. It would also have pointed out his aggression during placements, his bad absence record and argumentative approach to his tutors.

Since then a number of eminent people in the medical world have suggested that in the light of medical advances the convictions could be unsafe and that there are logical and medical non criminal explanations for the deaths. These suggestions have gathered momentum and in May 2013 the Criminal Cases Review Commission started to re-examine the case in the light of these suggestions and new evidence that would not have been available to the jury at the time. In February 2021 the CCRC referred the case to the Court of Appeal saying that in their opinion the conviction had a serious possibility of being unsafe. The Norris appeal is ongoing at the time of writing.

****

2002 ANTHONY HARDY

Anthony John Hardy was born in Winshill, Burton-on-Trent Staffordshire on 31st May 1951and was the youngest of four children. Nothing that pointed to him becoming known as The Camden Ripper in later life surfaced during an uneventful childhood. Academically bright at school and college he went on to obtain an engineer's degree at Imperial College London and had a successful management career. He married Judy in 1972 and they had three sons and a daughter. They emigrated to Australia and there the marriage collapsed. In 1982 the alarm bells rang in Australia when he was arrested for trying to drown his wife. The charges were dropped and the couple divorced in 1986. Hardy then returned to London and his life went off the rails. He lived on the street moving between hostels whilst drinking heavily at this time and spent some time in mental institutions having been diagnosed with bipolar disorder. Further treatment for depression, drug-induced psychosis and alcohol abuse was given in various psychiatric hospitals across London. He was becoming known to the police and getting convictions for theft and drunk and disorderly behaviour.

His first serious offence was in 1998 when a prostitute brought a charge of rape against him. The charges were later dropped through lack of evidence. In January 2002 a neighbour at the block of flats where Hardy was staying called the police after somebody had smashed her front door and scrawled obscenities on it. She suspected Hardy as they had rowed over a leaking pipe. Inside Hardy's flat they found a locked door and although Hardy said he had never been through it and didn't have a key the police found a key in his belongings and entered the room. There they found a naked dead body later identified as sex worker Sally White thirty-eight on the bed with cuts and bruises to her head and body. Forensic pathologist Freddy Patel examined the body and surprisingly gave the cause of death as heart attack. Patel was later to be struck off the GMC medical register in 2012 and banned from practising in the UK after a series of wrong diagnoses. Hardy pleaded guilty to a charge of criminal damage which referred to his neighbour's front door saying he was drunk at the time. He claimed no knowledge of how White came to be in the flat or of anything happening between them, again inebriation was blamed. Whilst in custody the police doctors transferred him to St Lukes Hospital, Muswell Hill a psychiatric hospital under section 27 of the 1983 Mental Health act. He stayed at the hospital until November 4th 2002 when he returned to his flat. A tramp looking for discarded food in wheelie bins on 30th December 2002 near Hardy's home in Royal College Street, Camden found two human legs wrapped in black bin liners. They were both female left legs so indicated two bodies. A police search of the area found arms, a torso and a foot. Hardy later said the other parts were hidden in Camden but none were ever found and he refused to elaborate. Once the body parts were found suspicion immediately centred on Hardy and his flat was searched on 31st December. The front door was open but the flat empty, in the bedroom they found the other torso. DNA named the two women as Elizabeth Valad twenty-nine from Nottingham and

New Zealander Bridgette MacClennan thirty-four .
Pathology put Elizabeth's death at between December
10th and 31st and Bridgette's between December 23rd
and 31st. Later photographs found in the flat showed
Hardy arranged all his victims' bodies in sexual poses
to photograph them before dismembering them with
an electric saw and disposing of the parts in bin bags
deposited throughout the Camden area.

An arrest warrant was issued for Hardy who
had gone on the run but was spotted in the cafeteria at
Great Ormond Street Hospital a few days later by an
off duty officer. He fought to resist arrest and
managed to knock one officer unconscious, stab
another in the hand and dislocate an eye socket of a
third. Backup arrived and Hardy was subdued and
arrested at the scene.

DNA evidence on the blood stains found at
Hardy's flat proved the two women had been there
and neighbours told of electric saw sounds coming
from the flat in the middle of the night in the past. At
the flat was a devil's mask that the photographs later
showed Hardy put on each of his victims before

taking the photos. There was also a glass bottle with the label 'Sally White RIP' a stack of pornographic films and videos and a good number of letters describing fantasy sexual encounters he claimed to have had that he intended to send to underground contact magazines. The walls of the flat were decorated with satanic daubing and cruciforms. He had also sent a friend the forty-four negatives of the photos he had taken of the final two victims. Both had devil's masks and baseball caps on them and a vibrator inserted in their vagina.

Hardy was charged with the murders of MacClennan, Valad and White (Pathologist Freddy Patel had been sacked by now and the 'death by heart attack conclusion quashed) In November 2003 Hardy received life imprisonment. In May 2010 the case was reviewed to take into account Hardy's mental state but the Judge kept the three life sentences and added a 'non release' whole life tariff. The police were said to believe in the strong possibility Hardy is connected to the cases of two sex workers who bodies were dismembered and thrown in the Thames and up to a further six unsolved murders that bear the same hallmarks as Hardy's MO and victims, but not enough solid evidence is available to directly implicate him.

****

2003 THE CHOHAN FAMILY MURDERS

In February 2003 Onkar Verma was getting very worried. Onkar lived in New Zealand, his sister Nancy who was married to Amarjit Chohan lived in London. They spoke by phone on a regular basis. Especially since Nancy had recently had her second child, a son. Husband Amarjit had a thriving export business and had recently flown Nancy's mother Charanjit Kaur over to help with the expanded family and especially Nancy who at twenty-five was 21 years younger than her husband. Onkar was even more worried because on the last call from Nancy she sounded worried herself. She told Onkar that her husband hadn't come home from work the day before and she hadn't been able to talk to him as his mobile phone was switched off. Something he would never do, especially with a new child in the household. Amarjit's company CIBA Freight based near Heathrow had told Nancy that he had flown to Holland for a business meeting. He had not told Nancy about this meeting. There was a suspicious voicemail on Nancy's phone. It was Amarjit saying he'd be back soon and not to worry. BUT, it was in English and Amarjit always left his messages in Punjabi. The most worrying thing was that any trip out of the UK by Amarjit was impossible as his passport was with the UK Government supporting a claim he had recently made for a residency permit. So how could he have flown to Holland for a meeting with no passport?

Two days after Amarjit's disappearance the rest of the Chohan family vanished. Nancy, her sons Ravinder and Davinder plus her mother Charanjit Kaur simply vanished from their home at 35 Sutton Road, Heston.

The police were alerted after a few days by the CIBA staff who couldn't contact any of the family. The police didn't take a lot of notice but were becoming a little suspicious when just a few days later a known business acquaintance of Amarjit turned up at CIBA offices with documents and a power of attorney signed by Amarjit. The documents stated that Amarjit had decided to leave England with his family and had handed the company to this new owner. The police were not too worried because Amarjit was known to them and had a criminal history of money laundering, plus it was not unusual for immigrant families to change their minds and return to their home country.

No one in the UK was unduly worried with stories emerging that Amarjit had financial problems and could be running from them.

In New Zealand Onkar Verma had had enough of hitting a brick wall with his concerns to the UK authorities and flew over himself. He was adamant that Nancy would have kept him abreast of such developments within the family business and whatever the police thought he didn't trust the documents at the CIBA offices. Making a continual nuisance of himself to the police until they finally entered the Chohan's home. Nothing was out of place and there were clothes in the washing machine, food on the table and the family clothes were left behind and nothing packed. The clincher to Onkar was that his mother's copy of the Holy book, Guru Granth

Sahib was on the table, his mother would never, ever, go anywhere without it, never.

Two weeks later a letter posted in France was received by relatives in London. In it Amajit confirmed the family was on the run and going to go back to India, the problem with the letter was that Amajit always wrote his letters to the family by hand, this was typed.

On 21st March 2003 the Yard's Serious Crime Group got involved, mainly because of Onkar's continual persistence that something was not right. That the family had been abducted by person or persons unknown was now becoming the main stay of the investigation but the families bank accounts hadn't been touched so what was going on?

In April things got bad when a pair canoeing off the Bournemouth Pier saw a body floating in the sea. It was Amarjit Chohan.

A full crime investigation was launched which unearthed a plan by two drug dealers to take over a business through which they could launder drug money. Their plan involved fraud, the abduction, torture and murder of six people including the Ghohan family to get their plan into operation. Amarjit's business had a turnover in excess of £5m, money that fifty-four year old Kenneth Regan and fifty-two year old William Horncy targeted. Regan had started work at the freight company and noted the opportunity it would give him and his drug dealing associate to earn large amounts from dealing and to launder it through the company accounts. Drug dealing was something Regan was already involved in. Kenneth Regan led a life of crime across London and in 1998 was convicted of possessing 30kilos of heroin, also of bodily harm of a police woman who he ran over with his car when trying to escape capture. He was sentenced to twenty years but turned super-grass against his former drug associates for a reduced sentence of eight years. He was out in three years but because of his grassing he couldn't go back into his old life as there was a contract out on him. He took a job with Amarjit Cohen's CIBA company as a warehouseman. Maybe Amarjit had talked about his previous brush with the police to Regan if Regan's past had been known to him?

On 13th February 2003 Amarjit Chohan travelled to Stonehenge in Wiltshire thinking he had a bona fide meeting arranged with a prospective buyer of his company by Regan. He was met by Regan, Horncy and their accomplice Peter Rees. He was abducted by force and driven to Regan's home in Wilton, Salisbury, gagged and beaten until he agreed to sign blank letters and record messages for this family. Regan would then later write in the blank letters text confirming that Chohan was handing over CIBA to him. The plan was to file the paperwork legally and then when all had gone through successfully to support the story that Amarjit had fled the UK by killing Amarjit and his family who would never be seen again. They killed Amarjit and on February 15th Regan and Horncy went to the Chohan house and murdered the rest of the family taking their bodies away in a hired van.

When Regan took the papers and the story of Chohan taking his family from the UK to CIBA the staff were a little worried but they knew that Amarjit Chohan had had previous tax evasion and money laundering problems and even served prison sentences for it so it seemed possibly true that he was fleeing further arrest.

The family bodies were buried on a 50acre farm in Tiverton Devon belonging to Belinda Brewin a lady friend of Regan's. Then fearing they would be ploughed up Regan decided to move them and returned to the farm with Horncy to dig them up. They were disturbed there by Belinda Brewing returning home and asking them what they were doing in her field and they gave her gave a lame excuse about metal detecting. From there they hired a boat and dumped the bodies out to sea. Unknown to them Amarjit's body surfaced and was found by the canoeists off Bournemouth Pier. He was quickly identified and at the autopsy sedative drugs were found in his body plus marks of restraints being tied to his ankles and wrists. Inside his sock was a scribbled letter with Kenneth Regan's name on it. The contents of the letter have never been made public but the police believe it was hidden by Amarjit once he realised he was to be killed. In July 2003 Nancy Chohan's body was found after being caught up in fishing nets off the Isle of Wight and her mother's body washed up on the beach in the Isle of Wight. The two boy's bodies have never been found.

Regan was arrested on 2nd August 2003 when the police made the connection between the disappearance of the family, Regan's power of attorney and Belinda Brewin's farm activities. Horncy and Lees were arrested soon after. All three were charged with abduction, false imprisonment and multiple murders in November 2004. They pleaded not guilty.

Regan's home surprised the forensics police team as it was exceptionally clean with new carpets and furniture throughout. But a single drop of blood linked to the Chohan DNA sealed his fate plus the letter in Chohan's sock which Regan failed to convince the jury was a police 'plant'. Regan and Horncy each got life, Lees a minimum of 23 years as only Amarjit's murder could be pinned on him.

2004 MARK HOBSON

A serial killer who carefully planned all his murders, Mark Hobson was born 2nd September 1969 in Wakefield, Yorkshire and lived with his parents and two sisters in Norton Street. The family moved to a larger house in Woodhouse Road, Exmoor where his father, a coal miner, became over manager at the Park Hill Colliery until it was closed in 1982. The family then moved to Selby where Hobson's father worked in the local coalfield and his mother took a job as a machinist. Hobson was educated at the local Heath View Primary School and then Staynor High School, Selby. School reports have him as 'quiet and average'

Hobson left school and worked shifts at Drax Power Station and in between the shifts took other work as a landscape gardener. In 1993 he married his childhood sweetheart after moving in with her and her two children from a previous relationship in 1991. His wife described him as a 'perfect husband.' Nothing pointed to the carnage to come. In 1998 he registered as a nightclub doorman and began working at a club called Kans in the Market Square, Selby. On New Year's Day 1999 he upped and walked out on his family without giving a reason and drifted into cannabis and heavy drinking. His wife's later police statement says 'There was no one else involved, he just didn't want married life any more. It was bizarre. I couldn't believe it. He turned to pot and drinking heavily. He never drank when we were married but now he got out of his face. He became like a zombie... His life just went completely off the rails' He regularly drank up to 20 pints a day.

In June 2003 Hobson was convicted of wounding with intent to cause grievous bodily harm and failing to comply with bail conditions, in July 2003 he was convicted for breach of the peace, in February 2004 convicted for theft and deception. He served 100 hours of community service plus two years probation, was fined £50 and then another fifty hours community service for those convictions.

On 10th July 2004 Hobson murdered his then current girlfriend Claire Sanderson twenty-seven in the flat they shared at Millfield Drive, Camblesforth.

He battered her head seventeen times with a hammer and strangled her before wrapping the body in bin-bags. Forensics later decided that Claire had been attacked in the living room and then dragged to the bathroom.

On July 17th Hobson rang Claire Sanderson's twin sister Diane and told her Claire was ill and could she come and visit her after work. When Diane arrived that evening she was beaten with a hammer after being tortured with a razor and scissors and sexually assaulted. When found her body was 'hogtied' with her left nipple bitten off. Police believe Hobson had eaten it. The ultimate cause of death was strangulation, her head was covered by a plastic bag, ligatures were found on her wrists, ankles and neck, she had been sexually assaulted and her pubic hair shaved off. Hobson had previously told a fellow worker that he 'had picked the wrong sister to marry.'

The next day Diane's boyfriend, Ian Harrison, who was a friend of Hobson's came to the flat and remarked on the bad smell. Hobson said it was a problem with the drains. He offered to let Harrison stay overnight, thankfully the offer was refused or we might be talking about another murder. The next day Harrison returned to the flat with the twin's father George and found it open with Hobson gone and the terrible scene inside.

On July 18th he murdered James Britton a WW2 spitfire pilot and retired railway supervisor and Joan his wife in their home in Strensall, York. Both were pensioners. The reason he murdered them is unclear but it is thought Hobson intended fleeing abroad and needed money and thought the Britons were wealthy and maybe had cash at home or he could steal their bank cards and take money out at ATMs. They had been married fifty-eight years with two daughters.

Hobson was now the 'most wanted man in Britain' and the media had been alerted and given pictures. He was arrested at a petrol station in the village of Shipton-by-Beningbrough near York on 25th July 2004 after being recognised by an attendant. He admitted the four murders at his trial and was sentenced to life imprisonment on 27th May 2005 with a recommendation that he never be released. The court was told that in 2002 he had stabbed a love rival five times in the chest in front of shoppers in broad daylight and somehow avoided a prison sentence receiving a community order instead. This lenient sentence was criticised during his murder trial in the light of what he went on to do.

Hobson lodged an appeal against the whole life tariff which was turned down because of the horrific nature of the murders.

Whilst on remand before the trial Hobson attacked the murderer Ian Huntley and threw a bucket of scalding water over him and was put in solitary confinement for three months.

The police investigation found handwritten notes showing how Hobson had pre-planned his attacks and also a shopping list for big bin-bags, tape, tie wraps and air freshener. Planning the attacks for summer time he had also included fly spray on the list. Another list of future victims included his girlfriend's parents and the parents of his ex-wife. They also found that he regularly posted on sex chat lines and had contacted one the evening before killing Claire Sanderson. Five women had replied.

At the time of this book he is in HM Prison Wakefield, West Yorkshire.

****

2005 MARK MARTIN

Mark Martin had an ambition that he often boasted about, he wanted to become Nottingham's 'first serial killer', and he did.

He arrived in Nottingham as a homeless drifter in 2005 and joined the homeless community quickly gaining a bad reputation for stealing money with violence and threatening behaviour. Martin was born in Ilkeston in 1981 and lived at home with his single parent mother. He was bullied at school and given the nickname 'Red' because of a birthmark below his left eye. His school records list him as violent and aggressive. He had a criminal record for assault, threatening behaviour, possession of an offensive weapon and robbery. He told his probation officer in 2002 'I am evil, how long until I kill?' He told many people he thought he would kill somebody someday and even rang 999 the day after he had spent the night in custody for trying to strangle his wife that he was 'having bad thoughts and was going to end up killing somebody and needed help.' He began to live with and socialise with Nottingham's homeless community going to soup kitchens and making friends of alcoholics and drug addicts. He stood out to those who organised homeless benefits as a misfit as he had no drink or drug problems, had a home in Ilkeston and appeared clean and well dressed. Although homeless he didn't need to be. By December 2004 he was living in a tent pitched by some old Great Northern Railway warehouses that had fallen into disrepair off Great Northern Close, London Road, Nottingham. It was a homeless community of mainly drug addicts seeking privacy from the police. Martin's preference for violence to take people's benefit money or take their drugs and sell them on made most people avoid him. The word got round to most of the charities working with the homeless that he was a psychopath and potentially dangerous and to be avoided.

Martin's first killing, Katie Baxter, was between December 31st 2004 and February 1st 2005. The exact date is unknown, his second victim was Zoe Pennick between the same dates, then Ellen Frith sometime between January 23rd and January 25th

2005. Forensics later put the dates at Katie between January 1st and 6th 2005, Zoe between December 30th 2004 and January 4th 2005 and Ellen on January 25th.

Martin gave 'no comment' to all questioning when arrested. An inmate on remand with Martin after his arrest claims Martin told him all about them. He says Katie Baxter had been picked up by Martin in the city centre, taken into Martin's tent on the waste ground and strangled before being taken into the crumbling ruins and buried under debris. Zoe Pennick was lured to the warehouse by Martin telling her he had 2000 cigarettes he wanted her to sell on in the community and they would split the money. Once there he strangled her and buried her beside the same wall as he had buried Katie. Ellen Frith was different she was strangled in a squat in Marple Square, St Anns, which was then set on fire. A police witness said 'Ellen had been smoking drugs with two other men. Martin was already at the squat and grabbed her in the kitchen and strangled her with another man, John Ashley. Ashley put her onto a sofa bed and set fire to the body whilst Martin put a drug needle in her hand and stuck it into her leg.' The remand witness said Martin had told him he killed Zoe because she had left a syringe full of blood in his bed and Ellen because she refused to lend him ten pounds.

The police had a slight problem as the bodies were not found in the same order that they were murdered. Ellen was found first in the burnt out squat on January 25th 2005. Police soon established who the body was and who used the flat which was in a block due for demolition with some still having gas and electricity working, Martin and Ashley's names were mentioned often by the homeless community, so often together with testimonies about Martin boasting about the killing that he and Ashley were arrested and charged with the murder of Ellen. Whilst interviewing homeless persons the rumour developed about other victims so a new line of enquiry was opened into the whereabouts of two missing persons, Katie Baxter and Zoe Pennick. The homeless community were very forthcoming and once the police established Martin had stayed in a tent at the Great North Warehouse they searched the area and on

February 11th 2005 unearthed the decomposed remains of Katie Baxter unaware Zoe Pennick's body was but a few meters away. It's amazing that a fingertip search of the area plus cadaver police dogs brought in failed to find it. Finally it was unearthed on February 16th. Police were convinced they had the prime suspect Mark Martin already in custody. The investigation was a difficult one as detectives had to untangle several deaths and several suspects with witnesses from the homeless community, apt to have a roving lifestyle without fixed addresses which complicated things. Once a witness statement was taken, that witness then had to be kept track of in case they were needed to appear in court to give oral evidence. The remand witness at first refused to testify against Martin in court but eventually agreed to attend under high security and anonymously. The trial was at Nottingham Crown Court on January 16th 2006. With many of the witnesses having alcohol and drug addiction problems the police were worried about turn out. However most of them turned up and spoke well. The jury took 21 hours to return their verdicts.

Mark Martin 26, of no fixed address was found guilty of murdering Katie Baxter, Zoe Pennick and Ellen Frith and sentenced to life in prison. The home secretary added a whole life tariff which means he will never be released.

John Ashley 34, of no fixed address was found guilty of the murder of Katie Baxter and Ellen Frith but cleared of murdering Zoe Pennick. He was jailed for life with a minimum tariff of 25 years before parole can be considered.

Dean Carr, 30 of no fixed address was found guilty of the murder of Ellen Frith. He was jailed for life with a minimum tariff of 14 years before parole can even be considered.

****

2006 RAHAN ARSHAD.

Yet another Manchester serial killer, must be something in the water around there!! Arshad murdered his wife and three children in 2006. He beat his wife Uzma to death with a cheap £1.99 child's wooden rounders bat by smashing it into her head twenty-three times at their home in Turves Road, Cheadle Hulme. Then he brought his young children, Henna six, Abbas eight and Adam eleven down from their bedrooms one by one and killed them. At his trial the judge told him his crimes were so horrific he must serve a life imprisonment sentence for each one. After murdering the family Ashad cleaned up, hid the bat in a garden shed, packed a bag and fled to Thailand. The bodies lay where they had been killed for a month before relatives broke in and found them badly decomposed. Interpol was brought into the crime and tracked Ashad to Asia where he was arrested on the Thailand-Malaysia border. He had enjoyed himself travelling to Phuket and then continuing to Kuala Lumpur, Malaysia but was stopped at the border. He agreed to return to the UK given the choice of standing trial here or rotting in a Thai jail whilst extradition was sought. He claimed that Uzma had killed the children and when he found out he killed her in a 'blind rage' and fled.

Arshad and Uzma had a bad marriage, they were first cousins and married in Lahore in 1992, it was an arranged marriage. At the trial Arshad alleged through his defence lawyers that Uzma had been having an affair with a baby sitter's husband, Nikki Iqbal and the close knit Asian community had ostracised her. Arshad believed this and was further annoyed when Uzma began to wear western clothes and attract the attention of men. When she went to Lahore for the funeral of her father Arshad sold the family home in Burnage, flew to Pakistan, dumped the children, filed fake divorce papers and went off with the proceeds of the house sale. So things weren't very happy between them. When he ran out of money and returned to the UK the family convinced the pair to save their marriage and supplied the money for the Turves Road home. Uzma wasn't happy at all and told people that she thought Arshad had it in his mind to kill her. On 28th July he took the family to Blackpool for a day out and told them they would be going on a holiday to Dubai. It was a lie, Arshad had not booked a holiday and had in fact booked himself on the flight to Thailand which underscores that the murders were planned and his escape route booked. When Uzma found out that there was no holiday to Dubai that evening a big row erupted and Arshad went for a 'drive' he later claimed to 'get away from his raging wife.' When he returned he carried out the murders.

In court he claimed Uzma had killed the children and he had reacted by killing her. His story of what happened changed many times under cross examination and the jury found him guilty on all counts. He is serving a life sentence with an all life tariff.

****

2006 STEVEN GERALD JAMES WRIGHT

Wright was known as the Suffolk Strangler. Born in 1958 in the village of Erpingham in Norfolk he joined the Merchant Navy in 1974 working as a Chef on the Felixstowe ferries. He married in 1979 and had a son in 1983. The marriage broke down and the couple separated in 1987 with Wright going back to sea as a steward on the QE2 which didn't last long and then had various jobs, a barman, lorry driver and fork lift driver. He had a second marriage that lasted less than a year whilst managing a pub in Norwich. He took another partner after getting a job managing another pub in Brixton, South London and had another child. He had a problem with drinking and gambling which led to his employment being terminated. He had large debts from gambling and more recently had declared himself bankrupt. He tried to commit suicide twice.

Hi last partner was Pamela Wright (same surname) who lived with him in an Ipswich house in 2004. He had previously admitted to using sex workers throughout his life and brothels in Ipswich were his regular haunts.

The murders began in December 2006 when the bodies of five women were found in different places near Ipswich, all were sex workers known by police to be working in the area.

The first was 25 year old Gemma Adams whose body was discovered in the water at Belstead Brook, Thorpe's Hill near Hintlesham by a walker on December 2nd. She had not been sexually assaulted. She was a popular girl when younger and from an affluent family but as a teenager she moved into the world of cannabis and then hard drugs which led to her losing her job at an insurance company and she took to prostitution to pay for her drugs habit

The second victim was 19 year old Tania Nicol, a friend of Gemma Adams who had been registered as missing since late October 2006. Her body was found on the 8th December in water at Copdock Mill just outside Ipswich. No sexual assault had occurred. She was also using prostitution to pay for her drug habit.

Victim number three was 24 year old Anneli Alderton found on the 10th December by a member of the public in scrub near the A14 at Nacton. She had been strangled and was 3 months pregnant. She had a temporary address in Colchester and travelled by train to Ipswich on 3rd December which was the last sighting before being found murdered. She had been a drug addict since 2000 and prostitution funded that habit.

On the 12th December the bodies of two victims were found, 24 year old Paula Clennel who had been strangled and 29 year old Annette Nicholls. A member of the public had found Nicholls and police discovered Clennel a short way away by helicopter heat gun whilst conducting the Nicholls investigation. Both were near the Levington turn off of the A1156 near Nacton.

Clennel was a mother of 3 living in Ipswich and originally from Northumberland. As a known prostitute she had been interviewed by the local TV news about the murders and said she had to continue to 'work' as 'I need the money, I'm a bit wary about getting into cars'. Her children had been taken into care sometime before and she had a history of being placed in referral units. She was a drug addict since 1998. Nicholls and Alderton had been posed by Wright in the Cruciform position.

Suffolk police named the murder enquiry Operation Sumac. They warned women in Ipswich not to work the streets and received offers of assistance from Norfolk Constabulary in the hunt for the killer. Commander Dave Johnson a senior investigator with the Met was drafted in to help and advise. The local investigator was DCI Stewart Gull. Gull revealed that the police thought that the women had been murdered elsewhere and the bodies taken to the places they were found although they had no idea where the murders took place. Initially 200 officers were involved and 400+ calls a day were being received from the public. As the murders grew the officers were increased to 500 local plus 350 from other forces whose main job was looking through 10,000 hours of CCTV footage.

On December 18th the police reported that they had arrested a 37 year old man in Trimley St Martin near Felixstow on suspicion of murder.

On December 19th they arrested a second suspect, a 48 year old man in Ipswich. On December 20th the police applied for and were given a 36 hour extension to keep the second suspect in remand for further questioning.

On 21st December they announced the second suspect named as Steve Wright had been formally charged with the murder of all the victims. The first suspect was released on bail which was later cancelled and no further action taken against him.

On December 22nd Ipswich Magistrates Court remanded Wright in custody to appear before a court on May 1st to enter a plea of guilty or not guilty. On that day Wright entered a plea of not guilty and the trial was set for Ipswich Crown Court January 14th 2008.

The police presented DNA evidence connecting Wright to three of the victims and fibre evidence connecting him to all of them.

On 21st February 2008 it took the jury eight hours to come up with unanimous guilty verdicts on all five murders. He was sentenced to life with the Judge recommending that he never be released.

SUZY LAMPLUGH LINK

Suzy Lampugh was the estate agent who disappeared in 1986 and was declared dead in1994 although no body has ever been found. At the time Wright worked as a steward on the QE2 and Suzy Lamplugh worked as a beautician on the same ship and they were acquainted. Lamplugh's father has told the press he was contacted by the Met investigating a possible link between Wright and Suzy as Wright's ex-wife had confirmed he had been on shore leave at the time of her disappearance and they had met after he moved to the Brixton Pub. The police will not discuss it at all.

****

2007 DAVID TILEY

Tiley, 47 had a history of sex offences and had previously served a sentence for rape offences and was being monitored by police when he killed his fiancé mother of five Sue Hale 49 who suffered a brain disorder and her carer, mother of two Sarah Merritt 39 in March 2007. Their bodies were found at Hale's flat in Southampton. Tiley was arrested in Swanage two days after their discovery. It transpired that Tiley lived with Hale's body in the flat they shared in Meggeson Avenue, Southampton for a week after he killed her by stabbing her four times. Tiley told police he had an argument with Hale on March 7th and she 'taunted' him about his past offences. When the carer Mrs Merritt went to the flat for a normal appointment to help Mrs Hale bathe Tiley tied her up with bed sheets, took £150 from an ATM with her card, returned, raped her and stabbed her twice. At Winchester crown court Tiley was given a 'whole life' sentence.

****

2008 LEVI BELLFIELD.

Well known for the murder of Milly Dowler. Levi Rabetts was born in 1968 in Isleworth, London to Jean and Joseph Rabetts, he is of Romani (gypsy) descent. His father had eleven children with three wives and died when Levi was ten and he and his two brothers and two sisters lived on a south west London Council Estate from where he went to Forge Lane primary school and onto Rectory Secondary School, Hampton and then Feltham Community College. Levi's first conviction was at the age of 14 for burglary, then at 23 for assaulting a police officer followed by convictions for theft and driving offences. By 2002 he had spent a year in prison and had nine convictions on file.

Everybody who knew him had the same opinion of him, he started off being a nice friendly individual and quickly turned nasty when it suited him. With his girlfriends it was similar but he turned into an evil control freak of a person. Each and every statement made to the police by his ex's said the same. DCI Colin Sutton who led the murder investigation told the press 'When we began dealing with him he came across as a very jokey individual but he is very cunning and violent and can switch from nice to nasty in an instant,'

Bellfield would search for his victims on the streets he knew well and used his Wheel Clamping Business as a cover. When suspicion first fell on him he was followed and seen driving round in his business van stopping to talk to young girls at bus stops, offering lifts.

Amanda Jane 'Milly' Dowler was just thirteen when she went missing on 21st March 2002. She was found dead in Yately Heath Woods, Yately six months later. Surrey police submitted a folder listing evidence connecting Bellfield to her murder and in 2010 the Crown Prosecution Service charged him with her kidnapping and murder plus the attempted kidnapping of twelve year old Rachel Cowles on 20th March 2002. He was convicted of Dowler's death by jury on 23rd June 2011. He stood silent throughout the trial and refused to go in the witness box.

Marsha Louise McDonnell was nineteen when she was beaten on the head on her way home in Hampton with a blunt instrument after getting off the 111 bus in February 2003. She died from her injuries two days later in hospital. Bellfield quickly sold his Vauxhall Corsa car within six days of the murder having paid £6,000 for it five months earlier. He never admitted it but police think he was sure that car had been seen in the area of the murder on the day of the murder which is why he got rid of it.

Kate Sheedy was eighteen when she refused to get into Bellfield's car and he ran her down as she crossed the road near the entrance to an industrial estate in Isleworth on 28th May 2004. She suffered multiple injuries and spent a long time in hospital recovering. Four years later she identified Bellfield and gave evidence when he was tried for her attempted murder.

Amelie Delagrange a 22 year old French student visiting the UK was found with serious head injuries in August 2004 and died that night in hospital. Because of the nature of the injuries police suspected it was the same person who had attacked Marsha McDonnell eighteen months later. Bellfield confessed to the murder whilst on remand.

Bellfield also faced two other charges. Abduction and false imprisonment of Anna-Maria Rennie, then seventeen, at Whitton in October 2001. Rennie picked him out in an identity parade four years later such was the deep effect it had on her. He was also charged with the attempted murder of Irma Dragoshi, thirty-nine, at Longford in December 2003. In both cases the Jury failed to reach verdicts.

In 2008 Bellfield was found guilty of McDonnell and Delagrange murders and the attempted murder of Sheedy. He was sentenced to life imprisonment with the recommendation that he never be released. He refused to attend court. In 2010 he was in court again charged with Dowler's kidnapping and murder. The crime pre-dated the other three charges by a year and was sent to the Old Bailey to be heard. He was found guilty and sentenced again to life plus no release. A trial on another charge of attempting to abduct an eleven year old girl by car the day preceding Dowler's abduction had to be abandoned because of newspaper coverage prejudicial to Bellfield's case.

In 2008 after he had been convicted police named Bellfield as being a suspect in quite a few unsolved murders and attacks on women going back as far as 1990 as well as the unsolved murder of his childhood girlfriend fourteen year old Patsy Morris in 1980. In his cell at HMS Prison Wakefield he started admitting many unsolved rape and murder cases which involved a lot of work by ten different police forces following up these confessions. No real evidence linking him with any was unearthed and the cases closed.

He also confessed to another prisoner that he was responsible for the murders of Lin Russell and her Daughter Megan in 1996 but his ex wife told investigators that the day of those murders was her 25th birthday and Bellfield had spent all day in Twickenham and Windsor with her, a hundred miles away from the murder scene. Police believed her story as a credible alibi for Bellfield.

Bellfield is in HM Prison Frankland, located in the village of Brasside in County Durham and is a Category A men's prison.

****

THE END.

Sleep well! Don't have nightmares!!!

Thank you for buying this book. If you enjoyed it please leave a review or rating on Amazon as that would mean an awful lot to me. Thank you.

To see more books in this series, plus the DCS Palmer Serial Murder Squad series, the Ben Nevis and the Gold Digger Series plus others, and to get updates on new releases check my website:

www.barry-faulkner.com

Whilst there you may also like to sign up to my newsletter and receive advance notice of new books, freebies, crime snippets, talk venues and Literary Festivals I attend and other interesting posts. You can unsubscribe at any time and it's all FREE!!

Take care and stay safe!

DCS Palmer books

Future Riches

The Felt Tip Murders

A Killer is Calling

Poetic Justice

Loot

I'm With The Band

Burning Ambition

Take Away Terror

Ministry of Death

The Bodybuilder

Succession

The Black Rose

Ben Nevis and the Gold Digger Books

Turkish Delight

National Treasure

———————

London Crime 1930s-2021 (factual)

UK Serial Killers 1930-2021 (factual)

Bidder Beware (Comedy crime)

Fred Karno   biography

Printed in Great Britain
by Amazon